The Death of a Loved One:
Life's Most Severe Test

The
Death of a Loved One:
Life's Most Severe Test

-President Harold B. Lee

Featuring important doctrines pertaining to life and death as taught in The Church of Jesus Christ of Latter-day Saints

R. Wayne Shute

With a foreword by
Susan Easton Black and George D. Durrant

Millennial Press, Inc.
Orem, UT
www.MillennialPress.com

ISBN: 978-1-932597-99-8

Cover design and typesetting by Adam Riggs

A Psalm of Life

Tell me not in mournful numbers
Life is but an empty dream!
For the soul is dead that slumbers,
And things are not what they seem.

Life is real! Life is earnest!
And the grave is not its goal:
Dust thou are, to dust thou returnest,
Was not spoken of the soul.

Not enjoyment, and not sorrow,
Is our destined end or way;
But to act, that each tomorrow
Find us farther than today.

Art is long, and Time is fleeting,
And our hearts, though stout and brave,
Still, like muffled drums, are beating
Funeral marches to the grave.

In the world's broad field of battle,
In the bivouac of Life,
Be not like dumb, driven cattle!
Be a hero in the strife!

Trust no Future, howe'er pleasant!
Let the dead Past bury its dead!
Act, -act in the living Present!
Heart within, and God o'erhead!

Lives of great men all remind us
We can make our lives sublime,
And, departing, leave behind us
Footprints on the sand of time;

Footprints that perhaps another,
Sailing o'er life's solemn main,
A forlorn and shipwrecked brother,
Seeing, shall take heart again.

Let us then be up and doing,
With a heart for any fate;
Still achieving, still pursuing,
Learn to labor and to wait.

-Henry Wadsworth Longfellow

Foreword

By Susan Easton Black and George D. Durrant

How do you write a foreword to such a magnificent and meaningful book as this? That is the challenge that we faced in approaching the task. All that really needs to be said about this book is simple and can be accomplished in two words: "Read it!" But wait—there's more.

Wayne Shute has lived his life well. He has been blessed with extraordinary capabilities which have been honed by much professional training and many varied experiences. In addition, he has paid deep and loving attention to matters of the Holy Spirit. These attributes have almost qualified him to write on the universally important subject of death. We use the word "almost" because until recently, he still lacked the crowning qualification, which finally came to him when his beloved wife died. It is sometimes said, "You don't know it until you can write it." But in some cases, you can't write it until you know it. This singular event finished Wayne's preparation to speak to us about something he truly knows—the tender subject of death.

This book is not just a selection of the perfect scriptures, stories and poetry used to illustrate and give a foundation to each well-chosen point. Nor is it the reasoning of Wayne's mind and heart that makes this book a profound reading experience, but rather it is the sweet emotional moments that come as one ponders each line and chapter of his inspired message. We could go into the details of the book, but Wayne has already done that. Rather, we will mention just a few of the many insights he brings to us through his inspired compilation of sacred material.

Wayne talks about the death of a loved one as the most severe test we will ever face in mortality. Building on Elder Boyd K. Packer's quote, "Behavior can be changed by teaching doctrine more than it can by teaching behavior," he teaches clearly the divine doctrines related to death and adds the flavor of his personal experience and the stories of others.

We felt a tremendous impact with each chapter of the book. We were particularly impressed with stories such as that of Dean West Belnap, a man we knew and one who served so well in teaching the gospel at Brigham Young University. During the last years of his service to others, Brother Belnap was afflicted with a painful brain tumor, yet, he kept his hand on the plow until the sweet end. We could point out other poignant stories, but you'll find them as you read.

Wayne brings the plan of salvation into perfect focus and explains the Atonement and its relationship to dying and mourning in a most touching manner. He loves the teachings of the Prophet Joseph Smith and includes three funeral sermons delivered by him; each helps us to focus on important matters about dying and the loss of a loved one. Wayne explains that we are all preparing to die and gives added emphasis to the life of Christ as a preparation for death. He has a particular love and affinity for the words of Elder Neal A. Maxwell, who continued to comfort others while dying a long and painful death. We appreciate the author's inclusion of Elder Maxwell's quotes which help us understand valuable lessons taught when death sometimes comes slowly and brings immense pain and heartache. We were particularly touched by Wayne's statement that a joyous reunion with loved ones is related to doing family history. It is insights such as this that make his book a treasure and a delight.

Wayne points out that we learn some of our greatest lessons regarding prayer as we prepare for our own death and seek the strength of the Lord in dealing with the death of loved ones. We were gladdened by the hope that we don't have to be perfect when we die, for Christ is there to help us.

As we read this book, we thought of the hymn, "Sweet Is the Work." This is a sweet book, especially for those who have lost a loved one or who soon will face this great test. We conclude this foreword as we began: "Read it!" In so doing, you will be comforted.

Acknowledgements

I express deep appreciation for many teachers who taught me from childhood and eventual conversion to the Gospel of Jesus Christ to cherish truth. To goodly parents, Church leaders, friends, and family members I express my love and gratitude. I hope, because I cherish the truth, they may take quiet satisfaction in knowing that they have influenced my life for the good.

In the beginning of the book <u>David Copperfield</u>[1], we read these thoughtful lines: "Whether I shall turn out to be the hero of my own life, or whether that station will be held by anybody else, these pages must show." Although many of us may think that because of our accomplishments we are the heroes of our own lives, in my case, I know I'm not. I attribute everything to a kind and loving Father in Heaven and His Son Jesus Christ. I add apostles and prophets and many, many friends and family members, too many to name, to the list of real heroes and express my deep gratitude to them.

I thank my friend, Randy L. Bott who, upon reading the manuscript, gave a strong expression of support and insisted that the book be published. I thank him for his support in many other ways as well which go far beyond the publishing of this book. I thank also Ryan Bott for the very professional and competent way he has attended to the many details associated with the publishing of this book. I thank Doni Jones especially for her careful and helpful reading of the manuscript.

I thank Susan Easton Black and George D. Durrant for their friendship and for the thoughtful and encouraging foreword they have writ-

---

1   Dickens, Charles, (1980) <u>David Copperfield</u>, The Franklin Library: Franklin Center, Pennsylvania, page 3.

ten. I hope that what is written in the book will match their thoughtful and complimentary words.

When my Lorna died suddenly, I became one of millions, even billions of people who have had to face "life's most severe test." I thank the many people who were supportive and kind to me at that difficult time; they encouraged me to stay the course. I think they knew I would, but having friends and loved ones who were confident in me is so gratifying.

Contents

Preface

On Time[2]

Fly envious Time, till thou run out thy race,
Call on the lazy leaden-stepping Hours,
Whose speed is but the heavy plummet's pace;
And glut thyself with what thy womb devours,
Which is no more than what is false and vain,
And merely mortal dross;
So little is our loss,
So little is thy gain.
For when as each thing bad thou has entombed,
And last of all, thy greedy self consumed,
Then long Eternity shall greet our bliss
With an individual kiss,
And Joy shall overtake us as a flood;
When everything that is sincerely good
And perfectly divine,
With Truth, and Peace, and Love shall ever shine
About the supreme throne
Of him to whose happy-making sight alone
When once our heavenly-guided soul shall climb,
Then all this earthy grossness quit,
Attired with stars, we shall forever sit,
Triumphing over Death, and Chance, and thee O time.

-John Milton

2   Hanford, James Holly (1953). The Poems of John Milton, New York: The Ronald Press Company, pages 99-100.

This book is written to faithful members of the Church who have fully embraced the Restored Gospel of Jesus Christ and who have "lost" loved ones or will at some point in time. The book will be a comfort to them because they will resonate easily with the doctrines and principles which have come to us through apostles and prophets of the Church of Jesus Christ of Latter-day Saints. The book is intended to help you pass "life's most severe test" which is how President Harold B. Lee described the death of a loved one. And indeed you are facing now or will at some time in the future face "the most severe test you will ever face." I know this from experience; I know about the pain associated with the loss of a loved one and the test associated with it. But face it we must and hopefully, with faith and determination, we will be able to move ahead to see the positive side of death, the learning side of it, and grow to be better people as a result of it. If we do make much of life after the death of a loved-one, we will pass "life's most severe test" which will be a source of joy for us and them.

This book is also written as a testimony of the truthfulness of the Restored Church of Jesus Christ as taught in the Church of Jesus Christ of Latter-day Saints. It is from the truth of the Gospel and its doctrines and principles that we derive our understanding of the Plan of Salvation and our understanding of the necessity of death as a part of that Plan. It is from these truths that we derive our courage and our determination to remain true and faithful and our hope as we press forward in our lives at the time a loved one passes away.

It is written also to those who are members of the Church but who have wavered in their faith. This book is an exhortation to them to become fully active and committed to the Gospel of Jesus Christ. Without such a commitment, there is little sense that can be made about death without doctrine found only in the Restored Gospel. Once understood, the doctrine can be a great source of comfort. Without the true doctrine, it is virtually impossible to make sense out of death.

If you find comfort and peace in the pages of this book, I will be very happy. The faithful Saints (and those who have struggled to become so) who have preceded us in death are happy on the other side of the veil, so there's no reason we ought not to be happy on this side.

A BRIEF WORD ABOUT
THE BOOK'S MAKEUP

For reader's interest, at the beginning of each chapter, I have included a poem, scriptural reference or a quote relevant to the particular topic discussed. I hope you read and ponder them for the comfort they are intended to bring.

At the end of each chapter, I have drawn out of the chapter a number of salient and key points mostly pertaining to doctrine. I have added this summary to help readers focus attention on the most important points discussed in the chapter.

IT'S TRUE DOCTRINE
WHICH CHANGES HEARTS

True doctrine has the power to transform lives, hence our emphasis in this book on the key doctrines about life and death as taught by prophets and apostles. When a loved one passes away, the only real comfort comes in the form of true doctrines. So, when a loved one is near death's door, or has passed to the other side of the veil, what a sweet comfort comes from knowing where we have come from, why we are here in mortality, and especially at the time of death, where we're going once we pass to the other side of the veil

Such is the case of a dear friend of mine whose story should be a great comfort to us all and which sets the tone for this book.

My dear and long-time friend was eighty-four years old and lay dying in a hospital bed surrounded by his grieving family. His life had been a productive one; he had been prosperous and had accumulated much wealth. He had a devoted wife, the mother of his six children who were also successful themselves. Two of his children were faithful members of the Church; they along with their siblings held their father in loving esteem. He was honored on more than one occasion by our country's top political leaders for his generous contributions to the country. He had been diligent in his Protestant church activities acting as guardian of the finances and supporting his church's activities with quiet dignity.

Being a devoted Christian for most of his life, he had pondered the great questions of life—where he had come from; why he was here on earth; and where he was going. As he aged, he was particularly struck with the latter question—where will I go after I die? This question dogged him for a number of years; he could not find answers to satisfy his soul. Finally, in an act of humility, he asked one of his sons who was a member of the Church of Jesus Christ of Latter-day Saints if he had given thought to these questions and if so, did he have answers to them. The son of course complied and had the comforting answers to the questions. Successful and somewhat dogmatic people have a hard time humbling themselves to ask such questions especially of their children. In addition to the wonderful and satisfactory answers, the son added, "Dad, it's time for you to give ear to the truth. You must delay no longer!"

So my friend listened with real intent; was touched by the Holy Ghost and was, ". . . spiritually born of God; received God's image in his countenance; and experienced a mighty change in his heart (see Alma 5:14). He was baptized and a year later was endowed and sealed in the temple.

A year later, he was rushing headlong to the grave, all the while his family members quietly watched and waited. They grieved—all but his faithful two children who understood the Plan of Salvation. Indeed, they rejoiced that their father, after so many years, had embraced the truth of the Gospel. While gathered at his deathbed, all the family yearned for one more expression from their husband and father who was slipping in and out of a coma. Finally, the moment came. The old man looked into the eyes of his loved ones and with a great effort, helped by a family member, he raised himself up on his elbows. Then with a voice strong and clear he said, "You all look so sad and worried. As for me, I am filled with happiness. I want you to know that before I joined the Church and went to the temple, I had no idea where I was going after I die. Now however, I know—for me the future is bright. Yes, I now know where I'm going."

His firm and strong expression fairly stunned the family. For the past three days he could hardly whisper—he had coughed a lot and often appeared to be choking. They didn't think he had the strength to speak with such power. But just before he passed through the veil, he was resolute and happy and had expanded insight into the Plan of Salvation.

Introduction

"Death of a loved one is the most severe test that you will ever face"

-Harold B. Lee

What reason have we to mourn?
None, except that we are deprived
for a few days of the society of one whom we love.
And if we prove faithful while in the flesh
we will soon follow, and be glad that we had the privilege
of passing through mortality, and that we lived in a day
in which the fullness of the everlasting gospel was preached,
through which we will be exalted . . . [3]

-Joseph F. Smith

THE SEEMING FINALITY OF DEATH

The grief and mental anguish that often accompany the death of a loved one are common occurrences experienced throughout the world, especially among those who do not have a testimony of the Restored Gospel of Jesus Christ. The pain and suffering that many people experience at the time of the passing of someone dear is touching, mainly because death so often carries with it feelings of fear and finality.

---

[3] Gospel Doctrine: Selections from the Sermons and Writings of Joseph F. Smith, Salt Lake City, Utah: Deseret Book Company, page 441.

In many places in the world, in a variety of settings, I have witnessed the sense of hopelessness which accompanies death, especially the death of a loved one. It is sad to see death's effect on individuals, family members and friends who do not understand the true meaning of life. In places where I have labored in Church assignments—Samoa, Armenia, East Malaysia, Cypress, and Greece and elsewhere—I have witnessed firsthand the pain, the despair, the agonizing anguish of family members as they try to cope with the death of a husband or a wife, a mother or a father, a son or daughter, a brother or sister. For most people, death is very difficult to face. I have seen a son, for example, throw himself into an open grave with a deceased father refusing to accept the finality of his dad's mortal life—all this, while dirt was being shoveled into the grave; I have heard the prolonged wailing of a wife for her departed husband. I have seen open coffins leaned against homes for extended hours as if to wait the departed one's return. These sad images and others are impossible to erase from my sympathetic memory.

For most people in the world, death is beyond comprehension—most cling to life with fear and trepidation of the future. And whereas those who have been terribly sick or afflicted, perhaps through illness or accident, yearn for death as their lives linger on, it is still never quite timely or comprehensible when they do pass away. In contrast, there are those who die suddenly, without warning; we are happy for those who die in their sleep or suddenly, yet, it is often more difficult for those who remain behind to comprehend the death or make an adequate adjustment to it.

Sadly, what adds to the finality of death in the minds of most people is the body of a loved one becomes cold, stiff and unresponsive—indeed lifeless. As people gaze upon the lifeless form of a loved one, they suffer and sorrow. It is sad to see what, in most people's minds, are serious doubts as to whether or not they will ever see the loved one alive again. And whereas it is true most people have some idea of an afterlife, it is mostly shrouded in mystery and obscurity. Even for those who have some religious inclination, there seems for most people little hope in the future of ever seeing their loved one again; hence, the intense grief at the death of a loved one.

Accompanying all of this is fear. It is universal that death or the idea of death brings with it intense fear so that when the time comes for a loved one to pass on, great sorrow and suffering attend it. Death raises so many questions—Will I ever see my loved one again? Where is she? What will he be doing if there is life after death? These and a myriad of other like questions are raised as loved ones pass away—the suffering and the sorrow are intense if there are no answers to these troubling questions.

SORROW FLEES IN THE FACE OF THE RESTORED GOSPEL OF JESUS CHRIST

Although there is sorrow when a loved one passes away, faithful members of The Church of Jesus Christ of Latter-day Saints realize that the soul is eternal, alive and well and that the spiritual body of a deceased loved one is just beyond the veil which separates mortality from immortality—a very thin veil. As President Ezra Taft Benson noted:

> I am sure many of you know that the veil can be very thin—
> that there are people over there who are pulling for us—people who
> have faith in us and who have great hopes for us, who are hop-
> ing and praying that we will measure up—our loved ones (parents,
> grandparents, brothers, sisters, and friends) who have passed on.
> (Salt Lake Utah Emigration Stake Conference, 2 February 1975). [4]

Faithful Latter-day Saints understand perfectly well that the spirit lives on, that there is a plan for mortals which extends beyond the grave. From mortality we move on to the Spirit World where spirit bodies of all mortals await the resurrection. The Spirit World is a place of learning, of active living, in pushing forward the work that we do here—that of building the Kingdom of God. It is a place of happy moments where there is a glorious reunion with relatives, friends and loved ones. It is a world filled with love.

Even so, facing the death of a loved one is painful and difficult. In the words of President Harold B. Lee, who was well acquainted with the grief that comes with the loss of a spouse,

> Death of a loved one is the most severe test that you will ever
> face . . . [5]

---

4   The Teachings of Ezra Taft Benson. Salt Lake City, Utah: Bookcraft, p. 31
5   Williams, Clyde J. (1996), Teachings of Harold B. Lee: Eleventh President of the Church of Jesus Christ of Latter-day Saints, Salt Lake City, Utah: Bookcraft, pp. 53-54

DEATH CAN BE A GREAT TEACHER

As is the case with all trials and tribulations of life, there is something important and needful we can learn when these heartaches such as the death of a loved one come along. There is always something very positive for us to gain from the experience of "losing" one close to us. When we can see the positive learning that accompanies death, whereas it may not be welcomed, it surely is an important time for us to learn eternal truths. As in life there is much to learn, so likewise in death. Life after the death of a loved can turn out to be one of the most productive periods of learning in our entire lives. It is a time to be more fully engaged in the Gospel than we've ever been.

Sadly, one of the problems of which mental health professionals warn us is that many people sort of "give up" and choose to withdraw from an active life style when they lose a loved one. I'm not entirely sure why this happens. Obviously they don't understand what the future holds when a person moves on to the world of spirits. Whatever the case, I am confident that "giving up" doesn't bring much happiness to either the ones who remain behind on earth or those on the other side of the veil. For sure, giving up at the death of a loved one will not add to our understanding of life or make anything meaningful of it.

The point of this is obvious—there is much to learn in life, and surely much to learn in death. In life, faithful Latter-day Saints make a sincere effort to be like the Savior, to try to be like Him, to constantly learn about Him. In death we can also learn much about Him—for sure we'll learn much more clearly about his atoning sacrifice for us when we pass through the veil. Not only do we learn a great deal about the Savior, but about many other things as well, especially about ourselves. Although sometimes painful, there are great lessons to learn at the passing of a loved one.

TRUE DOCTRINE ALWAYS
SETTLES ANY ARGUMENT

In this book, I have explored the doctrines associated with death. I was tempted to also discuss various ways to "keep busy" after the death of a loved one, but I resisted that temptation because once one understands true doctrine as in this case doctrines associated with death, behavior will change to be in harmony with the doctrine. It is in doctrine pertaining to death that we can gain great comfort. President Boyd K Packer's words make this point clearly:

> I have long believed that the study of the doctrines of the gospel will improve behavior quicker than talking about behavior will improve behavior. [6]

It's obvious that we must keep busy after the death of a loved one, but what is most important is to get true doctrine implanted in our hearts. When that happens, of course we'll keep busy—doing genealogical and temple work; being of service in the Church as well as to those in need; encouraging and teaching family members and doing many other things of productive interest.

To repeat, I believe that it is important that we have a sure knowledge of the doctrine as taught in the Restored Gospel of Jesus Christ. We must get the doctrine right. Then and only then will we have comfort and the assurance our loved ones are happy and alive in the Spirit World. I bear witness that if we follow prophets and apostles, they will teach the truth to us—it is from them that we obtain the true doctrine pertaining to life and death. It is to that doctrine that we should cling and hold on, especially at the death of a loved one.

When you think about it, the future is glorious for those who pass through the veil. Why wouldn't we be envious of our next step which is both a defeat for the grave and a wonderful victory for a loved one who has passed on. We should be so lucky! We should march forward with joy and happiness both in trying to prepare ourselves for our own journey ahead—not regretting the passing of a loved one—and living in such a way that when we too go through the veil, we'll have a happy reunion with loved ones and friends.

Much of Latter-day Saint doctrine pertaining to death comes from the Prophet Joseph Smith. Little can be said to improve on the clarity of his sermons pertaining to death (and life). He set the doctrines in place which haven't changed. Accordingly, in Chapter Four, I have in-

---

6   Packer, Boyd K. (1998). The Shield of Faith, Salt Lake City, Utah: Bookcraft, page 152.

cluded three sermons which Joseph gave at the death of friends. I have edited slightly these talks and removed a few sentences which don't pertain to death, but I have included the doctrines he taught about death. One of the most famous funeral sermons, for example, is the King Follett funeral speech which is a veritable wellspring of powerful doctrine that is so comforting. We should, as members of the Church, be ever grateful for the sermons and writings which have preserved many of the doctrines taught by the Prophet Joseph Smith.

In addition, many other prophets, seers and revelators and others have expressed themselves pertaining to death. Their pronouncements guide us, especially in times of sorrow and heartache. If we read and ponder their speeches and writings, we can learn so much and be comforted thereby—fundamental doctrines pertaining to the Plan of Salvation. It is particularly comforting to read funeral speeches where sound doctrine is presented pertaining to the wonder of the atoning sacrifice of Jesus Christ, the Savior and Redeemer of the world. Obviously, it is during funerals that great doctrine is preached and rightly so because it is, after all is said and done, the doctrine that brings us most comfort. It is in the doctrine that we can derive help in order to pass the "severe test" to which President Lee referred.

How grateful we should be to have the steady and inspiring words of modern day prophets who teach us eternal doctrines about life and death. For it is in these doctrines that we not only find great comfort at the death of a loved-one but also the help to pass "life's most severe test."

MAIN POINTS DISCUSSED
IN THE INTRODUCTION

1. Death, for most of the people of the world, is a time of fear, grinding grief, and sorrow.

2. According to President Harold B. Lee, the death of a loved one is the most severe test we will ever face in mortality.

3. For Latter-day Saints, even though death brings with it sadness and sorrow, it is a time of rejoicing in the Plan of Salvation and in the atoning sacrifice of our Savior Jesus Christ. It is through the Atonement that we gain great comfort and hope for the future.

4. The death of a loved one is a time of important learning and progress.

5. The veil between mortality and the Spirit World is very thin; those who are in the Spirit World are close by and from there can exert great and caring influence upon us.

6. There is much to learn about life when we have to face death.

7. The future is glorious for those faithful Saints who have passed through the veil.

8. It is in the doctrines as revealed by prophets, seers and revelators that we gain comfort at the passing of a loved one.

Chapter One
"All men are born to die"

-Joseph Smith, Jr.

. . . the elders of the church, two or more, shall be called, and shall pray for and lay their hands upon them in my name; and if they die they shall die unto me, and if they live they shall live unto me.

Thou shalt live together in love, insomuch that thou shalt weep for the loss of them that die, and more especially for those that have not hope of a glorious resurrection.

And it shall come to pass that those that die in me shall not taste of death, for it shall be sweet unto them;

-Doctrine and Covenants 42:44-46

NO ONE CAN STAY
THE HAND OF DEATH

Faithful Latter-day Saints understand that we are born into this world to die. In the words of the Prophet Joseph Smith,

All men are born to die, and all must rise; all must enter eternity. [7]

In keeping with the Prophet Joseph Smith's description of the inevitability of death, President John Taylor advises us that no one can stay the hand of death no matter how talented, how ingenious, no

---

7   Burton, Alma P. (1977). Discourses of the Prophet Joseph Smith, Salt Lake City, Utah: Deseret Book Co. p. 159.

matter what power someone may possess, everyone is going to die. And after the

> "enemy" which is death is destroyed, all the human family will burst the "barriers of the tomb" and "come forth." [8]

And we are reminded by President Joseph Fielding Smith that death is a crucial part of the great Plan of Salvation. He says:

> . . . death is just as important in the welfare of man as is birth . . . death is just as important in the plan of salvation as birth is. We have to die—it is essential—and death comes into the world "to fulfill the merciful plan of the great Creator (2 Nephi 9:6). [9]

President Gordon B. Hinckley said during the April 1999 General Conference of the Church:

> Those of us who live in comfort and security seldom give any thought to death. Our minds are on other things. Yet there is nothing more certain, nothing more universal, nothing more final than the closure of mortal life. No one can escape it, not one.[10]

Robert Millet and Joseph McConkie capture precisely the nature of death, it's fears and pains, in their book, The Life Beyond. Death is to them, a "universal commonality" meaning of course, that we all share its inevitability just as President Hinckley noted in the quote above. Millet and McConkie describe also the fear that accompanies death which may be why we would do most anything to avoid it. But die we must even though it is "life's starkest reality." Here's what they say:

> Life's starkest reality is death. Death is "a subject which strikes dread—even terror—into the hearts of most men. It is something we fear, of which we are sorely afraid, and from which most of us would flee if we could." It is a universal commonality, one thing which every mortal shares with every other mortal, this in spite of earthly status and accomplishments. Every man or woman is

---

8   Taylor, John, Journal of Discourses, 15:348.

9   Smith, Joseph Fielding (2001). Selections from Doctrines of Salvation: Sermons and Writings of Joseph Fielding Smith. Salt Lake City Utah: Bookcraft, pages 86-87.

10   Hinckley, Gordon B. Discourses of President Gordon B. Hinckley, Salt Lake City, Utah: Published by the Church of Jesus Christ of Latteer-day Saints, Volume 1, page 284.

born and every man and woman must die. All are born as helpless infants, and all are equally helpless in the face of death. Even
among those who see by the lamp of gospel understanding, death
is frequently viewed with fear and trembling. Joseph Smith is reported to have taught that "the Lord in his wisdom had implanted
the fear of death in every person that they might cling to life and
thus accomplish the designs of their Creator." The severance of
fraternal and familial ties is of all things most painful for those
who remain, bringing with it an avalanche of loneliness and sorrow. Such are the feelings even of men and women of faith. He
who has the panoramic vision and the broadest perspective on life
and death is aware of such agonies. The God of us all has said:
"Thou shalt live together in love, insomuch that thou shalt weep
for the loss of them that die'(D&C 42:45).[11]

I especially like the idea from Joseph Smith where he is purported
to say that we all have a fear of death so that we might "cling to life and
thus accomplish the designs" of our Heavenly Father. Their statement,
which goes along nicely with President Lee's sentiment, death is "most
painful for those who remain . . ." is touching and will be explored in
depth later in this book.

Though we all must die, we can be assured that Heavenly Father is
in charge of life and death. After all, it is His plan that we are born into
this life and that we all must die. All things are in His hands; and rightly
so, for mere mortals are not capable of managing such monumental tasks
of which life and death are a part. We have to trust Heavenly Father that
what is best for us will be done; we must bow in humility before Him
and acknowledge His hand in all things.[12] We can't give lip service here—
we can't as members of the true Church both second guess Him and at
the same time exercise faith in Him. This is too risky for our good.

SEEING DEATH AS A BLESSING

We all must die—there is no argument or confusion about that.
The argument and the confusion centers on the question, "Is this part

---

11   Millet, Robert L. & McConkie, Joseph Fielding (1986). The Life Beyond, Salt Lake
      City, Utah: Deseret Book Company, page 14.
12   Young, Seymour B. Conference Report, October 1901

of a grand plan?" Well, yes, dying is part of a plan which was put in place by a loving Heavenly Father—He designed it; it unfolds exactly as He wishes. We may not like parts of it, particularly the dying part, but it is what it is. His plan is the one under which we must operate— that's the way it is. So, acknowledging Heavenly Father as our loving Father with our faith fully and firmly in place, we are then in a position to treat death as a blessing. Once we comprehend the wonder of the Plan of Redemption and Salvation, we can't help but see death as a blessing, hard though that may be to understand. In the words of the Prophet Joseph Smith,

> The only difference between the old and young dying is, one lives longer in heaven and eternal light and glory than the other, and is freed a little sooner from this miserable wicked world.[13]

> More painful to me are the thoughts of annihilation than death. If I have no expectation of seeing my father, mother, brothers, sisters and friends again, my heart would burst in a moment, and I should go down to my grave.

> The expectation of seeing my friends in the morning of the resurrection cheers my soul and makes me bear up against the evils of life. It is like their taking a long journey, and on their return we meet them with increased joy.[14]

We must experience death in order to receive its promised blessings which are far more glorious than any blessings we could enjoy on earth. So, if we want eternal life, we have to die—it surely is well worth whatever difficulties we may have to face attendant to our death or to the death of a loved one.

The reason faithful Latter-day Saints take such a calm, even joyous approach pertaining to death is quite easy to see. In fact, we view death as a release from the problems and trials of mortality. In truth, it would be a tragedy if men were compelled to remain in mortality knowing that as they got older, they could not have the ability to en-

---

13   Smith, Joseph. <u>Documentary History of the Church</u>, 4:554.
14   Smith, Joseph. <u>Documentary History of the Church</u>, 5:362.

joy longer life on earth. President George Albert Smith comforts us in these words:

> And so the Lord has decreed that we all come into the world in the same way, our time here being limited. We all have an opportunity to enjoy happiness in mortality, and then, if we have been wise, we pass on, prepared for eternal happiness in the celestial kingdom when this earth shall be cleansed and purified by fire and will be presided over by our Heavenly Father and by our Elder Brother, Jesus Christ, as one of their dominions. With that assurance in our lives, death is not such a serious matter.[15]

President Brigham Young made a statement in which he said that when we have crossed over to the other side of the veil, it will be the greatest "advantage" of our lives because we will pass from our trials of our lives with all its sorrow, grief, mourning, woe, etc. into a state of happiness where we'll be able to enjoy life to the fullest. He goes on to say that our spirits will be free, and in addition, we'll not thirst, or hunger, or be fatigued, or be tired, we'll be full of life and vigor, all the while enjoying the presence of our Heavenly Father.[16]

DEATH FULFILLS THE GREAT PLAN OF HAPPINESS

It's a curious thing, though, that while we know we all must die, and even though there are so many prophetic utterances giving us assurance that there is life after death, people still experience pain and suffering when death strikes down a loved one. Many, if not most, are immobilized by it. And interestingly, even though all mortals at some time or another must face the death of a loved one, we often don't think that death will come to us or to someone we love, hence we are mostly unprepared for it when it does come.

---

15   Smith, George Albert. Improvement Era, June 1945.
16   Young, Brigham. Journal of Discourses, 17:142.

This is why it is so important to understand why we are on earth in the first place. President Joseph F. Smith reminds us why we are in mortality in the following:

> . . . We have come to sojourn in the flesh, to obtain tabernacles for our immortal spirits; or, in other words, we have come for the purpose of accomplishing a work like that which was accomplished by the Lord Jesus Christ. The object of our earthly existence is that we may have a fullness of joy, and that we may become the sons and daughters of God, in the fullest sense of the word, being heirs of God and joint heirs with Jesus Christ, to be kings and priests unto God, to inherit glory, dominion, exaltation, thrones and every power and attribute developed and possess by our Heavenly Father. This is the object of our being on this earth. In order to attain unto this exalted position, it is necessary that we go through this mortal experience, or probation, by which we may prove ourselves worthy, through the aid of our elder brother Jesus. [17]

With so much at stake in terms of realizing our eternal possibility, we ought to welcome the death of a righteous loved one, for they are fulfilling, even complementing, Heavenly Father's plan. We don't want to expedite our departure from mortality because there is so much of importance to learn while we are here, but on the other hand, we shouldn't fear death because we are fulfilling the great Plan of Happiness which is authored by Heavenly Father.

Once again, learning is key to our well-being and happiness. We are here on earth to be tested, so we go about our lives learning important lessons in order to pass the tests that come to us. Some of the tests are easier than others; some are very difficult—death being one of them. Life forces us into all kinds of learning—in some instances the lessons are painful, some instances not so painful, but learn we must from all of life's experiences. That's why we're here. So, when a loved one dies, we mourn of course, but we must learn from the experience and move on.

---

17   Gospel Doctrine: Selections from the Sermons and Writings of Joseph F. Smith, Salt Lake City, Utah: Deseret Book Company, page 439.

All that aside, death is inevitable and will come sooner or later—it is part of a great eternal plan. "Death is fundamental to our eternal progress,"[18] declared President Ezra Taft Benson and is one of the purposes "of man's mortal probation."[19]

> In death, the body returns to the earth or the elements from which it was created, and the spirit goes into the world of spirits— there to wait the day of resurrection."

President Benson directs us to comforting words sung in the Psalms and also to Isaiah:

> Precious in the sight of the Lord is the death of his saints (Psalms 116:15). He will swallow up death in victory; and the Lord God will wipe away tears from off all faces . . . (Isaiah 25:8). Even though death is inevitable, the above comments give us great hope in the future as we continue to progress. All our hopes, however, can only be realized through the great Plan of Salvation of which the Atonement is central. It is to that Atonement we now turn our attention.

MAIN POINTS DISCUSSED
IN CHAPTER ONE

1. All men and women are born to die.

2. Death strikes fear into the hearts of people, unless they understand the great Plan of Salvation as authored by our Heavenly Father.

3. When dealing with the death of loved ones, faithful Latter-day Saints will find great joy and happiness in the truth pertaining to the Plan of Salvation and Redemption as taught by prophets and apostles.

4. When death takes a loved one, he or she passes from pain, sorrow, and suffering into a state of peace and happiness.

5. Death is essential to our eternal progress and should be considered a great blessing; the greatest blessing is that we move forward

---

18   Benson, Ezra Taft (1988). The Teachings of Ezra Taft Benson, Salt Lake City, Utah: Bookcraft, page 32.

19   Ibid., page 30.

on the path of eternal progress which we hope will culminate in the presence of our Heavenly Father. Indeed, death fulfills the great Plan of Happiness.

Chapter Two
"As in Adam all die, even so in Christ shall all be made alive"

1 Corinthians 15:22

Wherefore, how great the importance to make these things known unto the inhabitants of the earth, that they may know that there is no flesh that can dwell in the presence of God, save it be through the merits, and mercy, and grace of the Holy Messiah, who layeth down his life according to the flesh, and taketh it again by the power of the Spirit, that he may bring to pass the resurrection of the dead, being the first that should rise.

2 Nephi 2:8

UPON THE CROSS OF CALVARY[20]

Upon the cross of Calvary, They crucified our Lord And sealed with blood the sacrifice, that sanctified his word.

Upon the cross he meekly died, For all mankind to see That death unlocks the passageway, Into eternity.

Upon the cross our Savior died, But, dying brought new birth, Through resurrection's miracle, To all the sons of earth.

IT IS UPON THE ATONING SACRIFICE OF JESUS CHRIST THAT OUR FAITH RESTS

On the passing of a loved one, faithful Latter-day Saints focus attention on the atoning sacrifice of our Savior Jesus Christ probably more intensely than ever before.

Hymnal of the Church of Jesus Christ of Latter-day Saints, hymn 184

Thousands upon thousands, even tens of thousands of books have been written on the subject of the atoning sacrifice of Jesus the Christ, for it is upon the universal coverage of the Atonement that we place our hope for the ultimate redemption of all of us. And because of the Atonement and all its promises, we have hope and assurance that our loved ones who have passed on will be covered by its universal efficacy.

Because of the atoning sacrifice, we have much to be grateful for at the passing of a loved one. We have the assurance, for example, that all who die shall go to the Spirit World where they will await the resurrection. We have the assurance that all mankind will be resurrected, all will rise from the dead—there is no doubt about it! All eternal things are made possible by the atoning sacrifice of Jesus Christ. The teachings of prophets and apostles make this very clear. Here's what the Prophet Joseph Smith said about this:

> 'As in Adam all die, even so in Christ shall all be made alive;'
> all shall be raised from the dead (1 Corinthians 15:22). The Lamb
> of God hath brought to pass the resurrection, so that all shall rise
> from the dead."[21]

This promise, the promise of resurrection given to each of us, is so fundamental to our religion as Latter-day Saints:

> The fundamental principles of our religion are the testimony
> of the Apostles and Prophets, concerning Jesus Christ, that He
> died, was buried, and rose again the third day, and ascended into
> heaven; and all other things which pertain to our religion are only
> appendages to it. [22]

We know as Latter-day Saints, that the Savior took upon Himself the entire burden of mankind with the promise of universal resurrection for all and, for those willing to keep all of His commandments in mortality, the promise of eternal life. For these two great blessings we are deeply indebted to Him almost beyond words to express. Jacob,

---

21   History of the Church 6:366 Joseph Smith
22   History of the Church 3:30 Joseph Smith.

though, in his clear and persuasive language, said what few are able to say:

> And he cometh into the world that he may save all men if they will hearken unto his voice; for behold, he suffereth the pains of all men, yea, the pains of all men, yea, the pains of every living creature, both men, women, and children, who belong to the family of Adam (2nd Nephi 9:21).

Faithful Latter-day Saints have the assurance, if they have been true and faithful to their covenants in mortality, they may enjoy the blessing or gift of eternal life. Elder Bruce R. McConkie explains the wonder of this gift in a short article entitled, "The Gift of Death, the Gift of Life." In his usual clarity, he links nicely the relationship between the creation of man; the Fall of Adam; and the Atonement of Jesus Christ. He says:

> Eternal life, the greatest of all the gifts of God, is available because of what Christ did in Gethsemane and at Golgotha. He is both the resurrection and the life. Immortality and eternal life are the children of the Atonement . . .
>
> But, be it remembered, the Atonement came because of the Fall. Christ paid the ransom for Adam's transgression. If there had been no Fall, there would be no Atonement with its consequent immortality and eternal life. Thus, just as surely as salvation comes because of the Atonement, so also salvation comes because of the Fall.
>
> Mortality and procreation and death all had their beginnings with the Fall. These tests and trials of a mortal probation began when our first parents were cast out of their Edenic home. "Because that Adam fell, we are" Enoch said, "and by his fall came death; and we are made partakers of misery and woe" (Moses 6:48) . . .
>
> And be it also remembered that the Fall was made possible because an infinite Creator, in the primeval day, made the earth and man and all forms of life in such a state that they could fall.

This fall involved a change of status. All things were so created that they could fall or change, and thus was introduced the type and kind of existence needed to put into operation all of the terms and conditions of Father's eternal plan of salvation.

This first temporal creation of all things . . . was paradisiacal in nature. In the primeval and Edenic day all forms of life lived in a higher and different state than now prevails. The coming fall would take them downward and forward and onward. Death and procreation had yet to enter the world. That death would be Adam's gift to man, and, then, the gift of God would be eternal life through Jesus Christ our Lord.

Thus, existence came from God; death came by Adam; and immortality and eternal life came through Christ.[23]

Knowing the wonder of the Atonement and what it means to us should bring inexpressible joy and happiness to our souls. The fact that "He is risen" means that we, at some point in time, will be risen also—how uplifting, how remarkable, how comforting to us! Much of what we believe and hold onto and gain comfort from as members of the Church of Jesus Christ of Latter-day Saints pertaining to the Savior and His love for us is captured in the wonderful hymn, "Be Still, My Soul" which I include below:

Be still, my soul: the Lord is on thy side;
With patience bear thy cross of grief or pain.
Leave to thy God to order and provide;
In every change he faithful will remain.
Be still, my soul: thy best, thy heav'nly Friend
Thru thorny ways leads to a joyful end.

Be still, my soul: Thy God doth undertake
To guide the future as he has the past.
Thy hope, thy confidence let nothing shake;

23   McConkie, Bruce R. (2003). This short article appears in a book titled, The Gift of Eternal Life: Favorite writings on our divine origins, mortal purpose, and eternal destiny, Salt Lake City, Utah: Deseret Book, pages 27-28.

All now mysterious shall be bright at last.
Be still, my soul: The waves and winds still know
His voice who ruled them while he dwelt below.

Be still, my soul: The hour is hast'ning on
When we shall be forever with the Lord,
When disappointment, grief, and fear are gone,
Sorrow forgot, love's purest joys restored.
Be still, my soul: when change and tears are past,
All safe and blessed we shall meet at last.

THE DEATH OF DEATH

We read the following very comforting words penned by Brother
Tad Callister in his book, The Infinite Atonement:

> What a devastating blow to death when Christ first unlocked
> the doors to the masses of imprisoned spirits who had so awaited
> the day of his triumphant resurrection! He arose from the grave
> "with healing in his wings" (2 Nephi 25:13) for all men. He
> opened the door that had been shut for thousands of years on
> billions of graves. He was the first to walk through that door, and
> then, in a display of unequaled mercy, he left it open for others to
> exit in a divinely determined sequence. John Donne captured that
> moment in these expressive lines:
>
> > Death, be not proud, though some have called thee
> > Mighty and dreadful, for thou are not so; . . .
> > One short sleep past, we wake eternally,
> > And Death shall be no more: Death, thou shalt die."
>
> With the resurrection of Christ, the long-awaited words of Ho-
> sea had come to pass: "I will ransom them from the power of the
> grave; I will redeem them from death: O death, I will be thy plagues;
> O grave, I will be thy destruction" (Hosea 13:14). Is it any wonder
> that Ammon and his brethren, who had a burning, unflinching con-
> viction of the future resurrection of Jesus, could face death again and
> again with no fear? The scriptures record, "They never did look upon
> death with any degree of terror, for their hope and views of Christ and

the resurrection; therefore, death was swallowed up to them by the victory of Christ over it" (Alma 27:28). Such were the feelings of the righteous of past ages: "All these had departed the mortal life, firm in the hope of a glorious resurrection" (D&C 138:14). [24]

ALTHOUGH WE HAVE COMPLETE TRUST IN THE ATONEMENT, IT IS MOSTLY INCOMPREHENSIBLE

On a recent trip to Jerusalem while sitting in deep contemplation in the Garden of Gethsemane, I tried to come to grips with the extent of His suffering—bleeding at every pore? falling on His face in agony? exquisite suffering? the greatest of all to tremble because of pain? to suffer both body and spirit? However deep my contemplation, however anxious to comprehend, I couldn't! What I do comprehend however is that it is real, it happened, just as the scriptures said it did.

I'm in good company when I say what happened in the Garden of Gethsemane is beyond my comprehension. Bruce R. McConkie noted:

> What has been preserved for us is only a sliver from a great tree, only a few sentences of what was said, only a brief glimpse of what transpired . . . There is no mystery to compare with the mystery of redemption, not even the mystery of creation. Finite minds can no more comprehend how and in what manner Jesus performed his redeeming labors than they can comprehend how matter came into being, or how Gods began to be. Perhaps the very reason Peter, James, and John slept was to enable a divine providence to withhold from their ears, and seal up from their eyes, those things which only Gods can comprehend. [25]

THE ATONEMENT COVERS EVERYTHING

In addition to the resurrection which will "pass upon all men," the Atonement has the potential to deliver us from the "awful monster"

---

24   Callister, Tad, R. (2000). The Infinite Atonement, Salt Lake City, Utah: Deseret Book Company, pages 172-173.

25   McConkie, Bruce R. The Mortal Messiah: From Bethlehem to Calvary, Book IV (1981). Salt Lake City, Utah: Deseret Book Company, page 124.

which we know to be death and hell. Nothing is more blessed than that!

Tad Callister describes the comprehensive nature of the suffering; there is no mortal condition which has "escaped his grasp or his suffering." He says:

> . . . voluntarily took upon himself not only the cumulative burden of all sin and transgression, but also the cumulative burden of all depression, all loneliness, all sorrow, all mental, emotional and physical hurt, and all weakness of every kind that afflicts mankind. He knows the depth of sorrow that stems from death; he knows the widow's anguish. He understands the agonizing parental pain when children go astray; he has felt the striking pain of cancer, and every other debilitating ailment heaped upon man. Impossible as it may seem, he has somehow taken upon himself those feelings of inadequacy, sometime even utter hopelessness, that accompany our rejections and weaknesses. There is no mortal condition, however gruesome or ugly or hopeless it may seem, that has escaped his grasp or his suffering. No one will be able to say, "But you don't understand my particular plight." The scriptures are emphatic on this point—"he comprehended all things" because "he descended below all things" (D&C 88:6; see also D&C 122:8). All of these, Elder Neal A. Maxwell explains, "were somehow, too, a part of the awful arithmetic of the Atonement."[26]

Brother Callister continues his litany of human conditions which the Atonement covers. He says:

> President Ezra Taft Benson taught, "There is no human condition—be it suffering, incapacity, inadequacy, mental deficiency, or sin—which He cannot comprehend or for which His love will not reach out to the individual." This is a staggering thought when we contemplate the Mount Everest of pain required to make it so. What weight is thrown on the scales of pain when calculating the hurt of innumerable patients in countless hospitals? Now, add to that the loneliness of the elderly who are forgotten in the rest homes of society, desperately yearning for a card, a visit, a call—just some recognition from the outside world. Keep on adding the hurt of

---

26   Callister, Tad R. The Infinite Atonement, Salt Lake City, Utah: Deseret Book Company, page 105

hungry children, the suffering caused by famine, drought, and pestilence. Pile on the heartache of parents who tearfully plead on a daily basis for a wayward son or daughter to come back home. Factor in the trauma of every divorce and the tragedy of every abortion. Add the remorse that comes with each child lost in the dawn of life, each spouse taken in the prime of marriage. Compound that with the misery of overflowing prisons, bulging halfway houses and institutions for the mentally disadvantaged. Multiply all this by century after century of history, and creation after creation without end. Such is but an awful glimpse of the Savior's load. Who can bear such a burden or scale such as mountain as this? No one, absolutely no one, save Jesus Christ, the Redeemer of us all.

All true doctrine which we teach as members of The Church of Jesus Christ of Latter-day Saints finds its root in the Atonement for it covers everything and assures us that death is but part of our eternal progression. The Atonement is a universal gift that covers Adam's transgression so that we mortals are not held responsible for it.

> The universal, infinite, and unconditional aspects of the atonement of Jesus Christ are several. They include his ransom for Adam's original transgression so that no member of the human family is held responsible for that sin . . . Another universal gift is the resurrection from the dead of every man, woman, and child who lives, has ever lived, or ever will live, on the earth. Thus the Atonement is not only universal in the sense that it saves the entire human family from physical death, but it is also infinite in the sense that its impact and efficacy in making redemption possible for all reach back in one direction to the beginning of time and forward to the other direction throughout all eternity. In short, the Atonement has universal, infinite, and unconditional consequences for all mankind throughout the duration of all eternity.[27]

The apostle Paul taught,

> If Christ be not risen your faith is vain; ye are yet in your sins. They also which are fallen asleep in Christ have perished (1 Corinthians 15:17-18) . . .

---

27   Holland, Jeffrey R. (1992.) <u>Encyclopedia of Mormonism</u>, Volume 1, page 84.

But the Prophet Joseph Smith assures us that He has risen! He encourages us with:

> . . . and if He has risen from the dead, He will, by His power, bring all men to stand before Him: for if He has risen from the dead the bands of the temporal death are broken that the grave has no victory. If then, the grave has no victory, those who keep the sayings of Jesus and obey His teachings have not only a promise of a resurrection from the dead, but an assurance of being admitted into His glorious kingdom, for, He Himself says, 'Where I am there also shall my servant be (John 12:26).[28]

We have so many pronouncements from both living and dead prophets, seers, and revelators that we can be assured that we will live after we die. The loved-one we have sent on his or her way into the world of the spirits has simply taken the next step in his or her eternal progression--very comforting indeed!

Here's another testimony, this one by President Gordon B. Hinckley. He says[29]:

> There is nothing more universal than death and nothing brighter with hope and faith than the assurance of immortality. The abject sorrow that comes with death, the bereavement that follows the passing of a loved one are mitigated only the certainty of the Resurrection of the Son of God that first Easter morning.
>
> . . . Whenever the cold hand of death strikes, there shines through the gloom and the darkness of that hour the triumphant figure of the Lord Jesus Christ. He, the Son of God, who by His matchless and eternal power, overcame death. He is the Redeemer of the world. He gave His life for each of us. He took it up again and became the first fruits of them that slept. He, as King of Kings, stands triumphant above all other kings. He, as the Omnipotent One, stands above all rulers. He is our comfort, our only true comfort, when the dark shroud of earthly night closes about us as the spirit departs the human form.

28   Smith, Joseph, History of the Church, 2:18-19
29   Discourses of President Gordon B. Hinckley (Volume 1, 1995-99). Published by the Church of Jesus Christ of Latter-day Saints, pages 103-105

Towering above all mankind stands Jesus the Christ, the King of glory, the unblemished Messiah, the Lord Emmanuel. In the hour of deepest sorrow we draw hope and peace and certitude from the words of the angel that Easter morning: "He is not here: for he is risen, as he said" (Matthew 28:6).

Finally, our current and modern apostles affirm the reality of the atoning sacrifice of the Lord Jesus Christ and should give us great comfort at the time of the loss of a loved one. These Brethren say[30],

> We testify that He will someday return to earth, "And the glory of the Lord shall be revealed, and all flesh shall see it together" (Isaiah 40:5) . . . We bear testimony, as His duly ordained Apostles—that Jesus is the Living Christ, the immortal Son of God. He is the great King Immanuel, who stands today on the right hand of His Father. He is the light, the life, and the hope of the world. His way is the path that leads to happiness in this life and eternal life in the world to come. God be thanked for the matchless gift of His divine Son.

MAIN POINTS DISCUSSED IN CHAPTER TWO

1. Death of loved ones causes us to intensely focus on the Savior's atoning sacrifice more so than at any other time and provides therefore one of the great blessings to those who remain behind.

2. It is through the atoning sacrifice of Jesus Christ that we will live again, all will be resurrected and, for those who are faithful to their covenants, they will have the opportunity to gain eternal life.

3. However intensely we study and ponder the Savior's sacrifice, it is basically incomprehensible—even so, it is a reality.

4. No mortal condition will ever escaped the grasp of the Atonement; every mortal condition is covered—it is universal in its breadth and depth.

5. Jesus is the Living Christ; the Son of God. It is to Him we owe everything—our faith, our devotion, our gratitude, and our future.

---

30   The Living Christ: Testimony of the Apostles, The Church of Jesus Christ of Latter-day Saints, 1 January, 2000

Chapter Three
"We must not demean life by standing in awe of death"

Sarnoff

> . . . blessed is he that keepeth my commandments, whether in life or in death; and he that is faithful in tribulation, the reward of the same is greater in the kingdom of heaven.
>
> Ye cannot behold with your natural eyes, for the present time, the design of your God concerning those things which shall come hereafter, and the glory which shall follow after much tribulation.

Doctrine and Covenants 58:2-3

THE COMFORTING ASSURANCE OF AN AFTER-LIFE

President Harold B. Lee, a man well acquainted with sorrow having lost loved ones to death, gives us in his writings much comfort and good advice. The comfort comes, of course, with the assurance that there is an after-life and understanding this helps us face the tests that may accompany the death of a loved one. President Lee puts this in perspective by rehearsing the wrenching experience which Mary, the Mother of Jesus endured.[31]

> . . . Huddled at the foot of the cross was the silent figure of a beautiful middle-aged mother. Cruelly tormented on the cross above her was her firstborn Son. One can hardly understand the intensity of the suffering of Mary's mother-heart, but she now

---

31   Williams, Clyde J. (1996). The Teachings of Harold B. Lee: Eleventh President of the Church of Jesus Christ of Latter-day Saints, Salt Lake City, Utah: Bookcraft, pages 49-50.

faced in reality the import of old Simeon's doleful prediction as he had blessed this Son as a tiny infant and said, "Behold, this child is set for the fall and rising again of many in Israel; and for a sign which shall be spoken against; (yea, a sword shall pierce through thy own soul also,) that the thoughts of many hearts may be revealed" (Luke 2:34-35).

What was it that sustained her during her tragic ordeal? She knew the reality of an existence beyond this mortal life . . . Heaven is not far removed from him who, in deep sorrow, looks confidently forward to a glorious day of resurrection. It was a wise man who said: "We cannot banish dangers, but we can banish fears. We must not demean life by standing in awe of death." (Sarnoff.)

As we learn from President Lee, the passing of a loved one is "life's most severe test." It is painful, as we all figuratively "huddle" at the foot of the specter of death when a loved one is taken from us. Of course, it is not like the death of our Savior, but it is painful nonetheless.

So, when a loved one passes away, how can we avoid "demeaning life by standing in awe of death?" From the scriptures and other sources, we learn the sanctity of life; we learn that death is not final—Jesus won over death by His suffering on the cross. In one sense, we honor Him by, of course, mourning the loss of the loved one, but not being devastated by it, or by being immobilized by it or being incapable of moving forward. What is important is to put the mourning into proper perspective.

As for mourning, President Wilford Woodruff put it into its proper perspective with a powerful testimony about being true and faithful to the Gospel of Jesus Christ, and when we are, there is no need to mourn. Faithful people move forward into the Spirit World free from pain and sorrow and free from the "power of the enemy of all righteousness."

In making remarks at funerals, which I have often been called upon to do, I have taken the liberty of speaking plainly my feelings with regard to the dead. And I will say here, when I see a man or a woman, a true and faithful Latter-day Saint pass away, I do not feel in my heart to mourn. Why should we mourn for the woman whose remains lie before us? She has been true and faithful to the sacred and holy covenants that she entered into with God her Heavenly Father; she has received those ordinances in the house of God that will prepare her to go into the presence of the best men and women that have lived upon the earth; she has left a noble posterity to bear her name and to bear record of and to emulate her example; she is freed from pain and suffering and the anxieties of life, and is now beyond the power of the enemy of all righteousness; she has opened her eyes in the spirit world, among her relatives has gone to enjoy the society of those who have washed their robes and made them white in the blood of the Lamb, and to inherit the blessings and glory of eternal life. No, I cannot feel to mourn for her.[32]

President Woodruff is so confident about life after death and helps us see its reality. Armed with the sure knowledge that Jesus overcame the sting of the grave, we can proceed in mortality with joy and happiness especially when we witness the death of a loved one. We surely don't need to "demean life by standing in awe of death" because our Savior overcame the grave—this is reality. And because of this reality, we aren't going to be immobilized by the death of a loved one.

I very much like the lesson we can learn in this regard from the life of Henry Wadsworth Longfellow as described by President Lee. As we know, Longfellow was one of America's most gifted poets. After his wife died, however, he became immobilized and was so grief-stricken that he could hardly face day to day living—he was tormented by his loss. In fact, for three years he desperately longed for her. As the months wore on, he simply could not deal with the fact that his love had passed away. He had no interest in poetry; he had "no heart for anything." In President Lee's words:

> Life had become an empty dream. But this could not go on, he told himself. He was letting the days slip by, nursing his despondency. Life was not an empty dream. He must be up and doing. Let the past bury its dead.[33]

---

32   Woodruff, Wilford, <u>Journal of Discourses</u>, 22:348, January 29, 1882.
33   Williams, <u>Ibid.</u>, page 53

It was in this depth of despondency that Longfellow came to the realization that there is more to life than death. Being so motivated, he began to write "the Psalm of Life"[34] three stanzas of which I quote below. The complete poem is quoted at the beginning of this book, but the few lines of verse below capture the essence of his thought pertaining to the loss of his loved one:

> Tell me not, in mournful numbers,
> Life is but an empty dream!—
> For the soul is dead that slumbers,
> And things are not what they seem.
>
> Life is real! Life is earnest!
> And the grave is not its goal;
> Dust thou art, to dust returnest,
> Was not spoken of the soul.
>
> Let us then be up and doing,
> With a heart for any fate;
> Still achieving, still pursuing,
> Learn to labor and to wait.

Longfellow wrote these verses and titled the poem, "The Psalm of Life." He put the poem aside at first, unwilling to show it to anyone. As he later explained,

> It was a voice from my inmost heart, at a time when I was rallying from depression.[35]

In a sense, Longfellow had allowed himself to "demean life by standing in awe of death." Death is not the victor in mortality; it is only a passing experience which we all must face sooner or later. For some it is sooner, for some it is later. It really matters little. Indeed, the length of mortal life is not what is mainly crucial.

> Those who lose infants have no need to mourn, because that child has achieved the purpose of life. Whether they live to the age

---

34   Williams, <u>Ibid</u>., page 53
35   Williams, <u>Ibid</u>., page 53-54

of a tree or die as an infant is not a prime factor, as long as they have completed the mission that the Lord has appointed; and that is our mission, to live out life and not to shorten it.[36]

THE MANNER OF DEATH MAKES LITTLE DIFFERENCE.

From the writings of President John Taylor, we read that the mode and manner of our exit matters little. He says:

> God, in his eternal decrees, has ordained that all men must die, but as to the mode and manner of our exit, it matters very little.[37]

President Taylor elaborates on this idea in the following:

> Since the organization of the world, myriads have come and have taken upon themselves bodies, and they have passed away, generation after generation, into another state of existence. And it is so today. And I suppose while we are mourning the loss of our friend, others are rejoicing to meet him behind the veil; and while he has left us, others are coming into the world at the same time, and probably in this our territory. There is a continuous change, an ingress of beings into the world and an egress out of it . . .[38]

So what is important here is not the length of one's life, nor the manner in which death strikes, men come and go, what is important is that we deal with death in the way the Lord would have. What is important is the courage, the faith, the confidence with which we face death of loved ones. One can only marvel at the courage of the early saints as they crossed the plains, as they buried their young and their old:

> Why should we mourn or think our lot is hard?
> Tis not so, all is right.
> Why should we think to earn a great reward,

---

36   Williams, Ibid., page 51
37   Taylor, John, Journal of Discourses 17:131.
38   Durham, G. Homer (1987), The Gospel Kingdom: Selections from the writings and discourses of John Taylor, Third President of the Church of Jesus Christ of Latter-day Saints. Salt Lake City, Utah: Bookcraft, page 22.

If we now, shun the fight?
Gird up your loins, fresh courage take,
Our God will never us forsake
And soon we'll have this tale to tell—
All is well, all is well.

WALKING OUT OF THE SHADOWS OF DEATH

President Lee has described for us how he dealt with the loss of his spouse. His story is helpful as we face the death of a loved one. He tells of the time when he was agonizing over the death of his spouse, when a non-member friend with whom he had been in business, tried to comfort him. His friend told him of the time when he lost his spouse. His friend said:

> Now, I want to tell something. I'm a much older man than you. Thirty-four years ago the telephone rang at the bank where I was the president. The message was that my wife had been critically injured in an automobile accident. Immediately, I said, "Oh, God wouldn't let anything happen to this sweetheart of mine— she is so wonderful, so lovely, so beautiful. But within an hour word came again that she was dead. And then my heart cried out, 'I want to die; I don't want to live; I want to hear her voice.' But I didn't die, and I didn't hear her voice. And then I sat down to try to speculate. What can be the meaning of such loneliness and such tragedy that stalks the path of all of us? And the thought came to me that this is the most severe test you'll ever be required to face in life. And if you can pass it, there isn't any other test that you won't be able to pass."

President Lee, on hearing this and when he returned to Salt Lake City began, as he said, to "walk out of the shadows." A verse came to him from Hebrews 5:8-9:

> Though he were a Son, yet learned he obedience by the things which he suffered; and being made perfect, he became the author of eternal salvation unto all them that obey him.

In this story told by President Lee and in contemplating this scripture, we can come to see how important it is not to let death win our hearts and minds. Rather we can be assured that if we conquer death's devastation, we can move forward and conquer other challenges and trials that come along in life. Dealing with the death of a loved one will not likely end the challenges we will later face; we may have to face the death of another loved one, or more. Death doesn't bring the end to our trials and difficulties. Knowing this, we must face the future with confidence and joy.

Once again we come to the realization that it is our testimony of the Restored Gospel of Jesus Christ that will sustain us as we move forward. Out of the very worst scenario related to death, we can look to the scriptures for guidance and succor. Here is Job's testimony who was struck down "without cause" (see Job 2:2) and suffered horribly—the reality of death was all around him. But he weathered the storm of death and came out of it all with a most inspiring testimony.

> For I know that my redeemer liveth, and that he shall stand in the latter day upon the earth;
>
> And though after my skin worms destroy this body, yet in my flesh shall I see God;
>
> Whom I shall see for myself, and mine eyes shall behold, and not another; though my reins be consumed within me (see Job 19:25-27).

All of this is to suggest that when we face death squarely and move forward with dignity and joy, we will be refined in the process. We become better people with stronger testimonies of the truth of the Gospel. We become better in the sense that we have not "demeaned our lives by standing in awe of death."

Said another way, adversity, tragedy and tribulation are part of our mortal existence, they are tests for us, not that we want them and not that God necessarily wants us to have them. However, the nature of mortality is that we cannot escape these trials of life—they go with the territory, so to speak. The question is not if we will have to face adversity, but when. Once afflicted, of whatever kind especially the death of a loved one, we then must prove ourselves without losing or compromising our faith and love for our Heavenly Father or His Son Jesus Christ. If we look upon adversity as part of our schooling in mortality, then there are important lessons to be learned from it.From experience, I know this is not easy—it is just the way it is! In the mean time, we must never "demean life by standing in awe of death."

MAIN POINTS DISCUSSED IN CHAPTER THREE

1. From the scriptures and prophetic utterances, we learn that the Savior's atoning sacrifice won over death and the grave.

2. Mourning the loss of loved ones is entirely appropriate and necessary for many reasons, but we ought not to be devastated or immobilized by their passing. We don't mourn much for the faithful Saints of God, knowing that they are in the Spirit World in the presence of dear family members, all moving forward in fulfilling the great Plan of Salvation.

3. We can be assured that if we pass the difficult test of losing loved ones, we will be able to meet other challenges in life.

4. If we look upon adversity (tragedy, trials, tribulation) as a part of our schooling in mortality, then we can learn important lessons pertaining to it.

5. One way to avoid demeaning our "lives by standing in awe of death" is to rejoice and be happy in the revealed knowledge we have as members of the Church of Jesus Christ of Latter-day Saints.

Chapter Four
So, what is the severe test that comes to us after we lose a loved one?

The Road Not Taken[39]

Two roads diverged in a yellow wood,
And sorry I could not travel both
And be one traveller, long I stood
And looked down one as far as I could
To where it bent in the undergrowth;

Then took the other, as just as fair,
And having perhaps the better claim,
Because it was grassy and wanted wear;
Though as for that the passing there
Had worn them really about the same,

And both that morning equally lay
In leaves no step had trodden black.
Oh, I kept the first for another day!
Yet knowing how way leads on to way,
I doubted if I should ever come back.

I shall be telling this with a sigh
Somewhere ages and ages hence:
Two roads diverged in a wood, and I—
I took the one less travelled by,
And that has made all the difference.

---

39   Frost, Robert (1952). <u>A Little Treasury of Modern Poetry: English and American</u>. New York: Charles Scribner and Sons, page 137.

THE TEST CENTERS IN THE RESTORED GOSPEL OF JESUS CHRIST

We have all heard, at some time or another, that life's a test; and of course we have before us President Harold B. Lee's statement that the loss of a loved one is life's most "severe test." In this chapter, I will suggest that although we have many tests in mortality generally, the most severe test we face in relation to the death of a loved-one is to understand, believe and have faith in the Restored Gospel of Jesus Christ. If we do, then we believe and have faith in the Plan of Salvation, Redemption and Happiness; in short, to maintain and increase our faith in the Savior. That's it! That's the severe test!

I'm reminded of a short anecdote told me by a friend. A young boy got ready for bed and then went into the living room to say goodnight to his parents. They kissed him goodnight and the little boy trotted off to bed. Shortly after the parents heard a loud thump; the father went immediately to the boy's room and asked the boy what had happened. The little boy said that he had fallen out of bed. The father asked, "How did that happen?" The little boy responded, "I wasn't all the way in."

In this chapter, I will emphasize the importance of being "all the way in" pertaining to our commitment to the Gospel. Although I will discuss other mortal tests in this chapter, my primary focus here is on our understanding, believing and having faith in the Plan of Salvation as revealed to us in the Restored Gospel of Jesus Christ. We have a choice, as Robert Frost has said in his famous poem, "The Road Not Taken" which I have included above, either to accept the Restored Gospel as being true or reject it either through apathy, disinterest or rebellion.

In addition, we must understand that all of us, before the death of a loved one, and after, will be called upon, sooner or later, to face tests in mortality of one kind or another. People who are soon to pass away aren't the only ones who must face illness and death. It may be that during the illness of a loved one, prior to his or her death, that we ourselves might suffer some malady. Then too, after a loved one has passed away, we may, even during the mourning period, suffer illness. The point of this is that in all stages of life we can expect to have some sort of tribulation, some kind of suffering. In a way, this may seem harsh, but we are in mortality to learn about Heavenly Father's Plan for us; we must learn the truths of eternity and mortality with all its trials, afflictions, and tribulations is the perfect place for us to learn about these eternal things. There is no end in mortality to the instruction we need for our future. Thus, there is no end to affliction.

THE STORY OF JOB IS INSTRUCTIVE

Let's consider the story of Job in more detail than in the previous chapter and use this story to fashion a number of important principles pertaining to trials and tribulation, or tests. Job is the classic example of a good person who suffered unspeakable pain. However:

> His ability to see beyond the pain of the moment has become a glorious lesson for us all—the lesson of remaining faithful during our personal Gethsemane. The first verse of the Book of Job in the Old Testament describes Job as a "man perfect and upright, and one who feared God, and eschewed evil (Job 1:1). He did not do anything wrong and yet in one day he lost all of his oxen, sheep, camels and, worst of all, his seven sons and three daughters in a tragic accident (Job 1:15-19) . . . He later suffered boils and all manner of sicknesses and disease, the loss of friends and the consternation of his wife, but he continued faithful to the end declaring,
>
> For I know that my Redeemer liveth, and that he shall stand at the latter day upon the earth:
>
> And though after my skin worms destroy my body, yet in my flesh shall I see God . . . (Job 19:25-26).[40]

As in the case of Job, bad things often happen to good people. Whether good or bad, we all will be tested to see if we will fulfill the purpose for which we have come to mortality in the first place—the

---

40   Shute, R. Wayne 006) Clay in the Master's Hands. See Chapter 8 by Christianson, Jack R. Chapter 8, "The Old Testament: A Handbook for Dealing with Adversity," page 132).

purpose being to see whether we will be obedient to God's commandments as restored through prophets and apostles. That's the key! Even in the face of severe trials and tribulations, we must learn to be obedient to God and his commandments as revealed to prophets, seers and revelators. And even though we choose to keep all the commandments, we will still have to face tests and trials—that's the nature of life, all of which is good for us.

OUR SUFFERING HELPS US TO UNDERSTAND THE SAVIOR'S SUFFERING

One writer suggests that suffering is a necessary part of mortality because it allows us to more fully understand the suffering of our Savior. Obviously, our suffering is infinitesimal compared to His, but nonetheless, through our own suffering we can at least appreciate in a small way His suffering.

> The teachings of the restored Gospel of Jesus Christ give us some understanding of the seeming randomness of mortality. We know that our Father's work and glory is to bring to pass our immortality and eternal life, or the kind of life that God has. An essential element, perhaps even the essential element of Godhood is compassion. The scriptures teach that the Savior suffered 'pains and afflictions of every kind' in order to learn how to have compassion for us. We, too, must suffer to learn compassion. Hence, it was essential that our Father place us in a mortal, fallen world to give us a context for suffering . . .

> . . . So, in reality our Father's greatest gift to us in mortality is to allow us to suffer, for by suffering we learn compassion, place us on a path to learn to love as He loves, which will ensure eternal life and immortality.[41]

---

41   Shute, Christian W. "Suffering: Our Father's Perfect Gift." (See Chapter Four in <u>Clay in the Master's Hands: Understanding Tragedy, Trials and Tribulation</u>) Orem, Utah: Millennial Press, pages 66, 76.

WE ALL HAVE TO FACE THE
TEST SOONER OR LATER

So, in a general way, as we sojourn through mortality, sooner or later, we'll have to face various trials which are designed to test us. We read from President Lee:

> . . . there's a testing for every human soul. And there's a test every year, every month in the year, for the Saints of the Most High God. And their blessing and progress will depend only upon whether or not they pass the test.[42]

President Lee makes it clear that we can't live on borrowed light either. We all have to face and pass the tests of life which will come as surely as the sun rises in the east and sets in the west. President Lee then quotes the following words spoken by President Heber C. Kimball:

> We think we are secure here in the chambers of the everlasting hills, where we can close those few doors of the canyons against mobs and persecutors, the wicked and the vile, who have always beset us with violence and robbery, but I want to say to you, my brethren, the time is coming when we will be mixed up in these now peaceful valleys to that extent that it will be difficult to tell the face of a Saint from the face of an enemy to the people of God . . . Then, brethren, look out for the great sieve, for there will be a great sifting time, and many will fall; for I say unto you there is a test, a TEST, a TEST coming, and who will be able to stand? . . .

> Let me say to you, that many of you will see the time when you will have all the trouble, trial and persecution that you can stand, and plenty of opportunities to show that you are true to God and his work. This Church has before it many close places through which it will have to pass before the work of God is crowned with victory. To meet the difficulties that are coming, it will be necessary for you to have a knowledge of the truth of the work for yourselves. The difficulties will be of such a character that the man or woman who does not possess this personal knowledge or witness will fall. If you have not got the testimony, live right

---

42   Williams, Clyde J. (1006) The Teachings of Harold B. Lee, Eleventh President of the Church of Jesus Christ of Latter-day Saints. Salt Lake City, Utah: Bookcraft, page 143.

and call upon the Lord and cease not till you obtain it. If you do
not you will not stand.

> Remember these sayings, for many of you will live to see them
> fulfilled. The time will come when no man [nor] woman will be
> able to endure on borrowed light. Each will have to be guided by
> the light within himself.[43]

There just doesn't seem too much wiggle room here—Latter-day
Saints must gain a bright and burning testimony of the Restoration
and its truthfulness and stand up to the tests of the world which, without doubt, are increasing for members of the Church all of the time.

The question is not whether or not we are going to face tests—
that's a given—adversity in the form of the test is our lot in life. So, the
question is not **if** but **when** will tribulation zero in on me? And when
these tests do come, how will I deal with them? When death comes,
how will I deal with it? Or, if I am now facing adversity and tribulation,
how well am I dealing with it?

If we accept the fact that we are being tested when tribulation
comes our way, even tribulation beyond our control, we might prepare
ourselves for the test. And, from time to time, Heavenly Father may ask
us how we are dealing with it. He might ask us for an on-going report
as to how we are meeting the challenge of mortal adversity. He might
very well say to us as he said to Adam in the Garden of Eden, "Adam,
where art thou?" or in other words, "where art thou in terms of main-
taining your faith in me as you face the tests of mortality?"

EVERY MAN PLAYS THE ROLE OF
ADAM AND MUST FACE ADAM'S TEST

These sorts of questions are part of a short story written by Martin
Buber, a German Hasidic philosopher/scholar. Buber, as is true with other Hasidic scholars, was a master story teller who taught Jewish thought
through the powerful medium of story. As the story, "Heart-Searched"[44]

---

43   (Quoted in Orson F. Whitney, Life of Heber C. Kimball, Collector's Edition, Salt Lake
City: Bookcraft, 1992, pp. 446, 449-50).

44   Buber, Martin (1958). The Way of Man: according to the teachings of Hasidism, with
a forward by Maurice Friedman, pp. 8-11. New York: The Horizon Press

unfolds, Buber makes a wonderful point of the Garden of Eden story to show that when He, God, called out "Adam, where art thou?" he knew where Adam was, but he asked the question to see if Adam knew where he was! So it is with us as we face the tests of life. He knows where we are; He knows we are suffering and He knows how well we are handling it. The question, however, is intended to help us see where we are in dealing with the tests of life, and to remind us of our relationship with Him and that there is a purpose in meeting the challenges we may be facing.

The main character of Buber's story is Rabbi Shneur Zalman, who was the rabbi of northern White Russia and who was put in jail in St. Petersburg because his enemies had denounced his way of living before the government. He was imprisoned and was awaiting trial when the jail keeper entered his cell thinking perhaps that he might have a bit of sport with the old rabbi.

The jail keeper began to converse with Rabbi Zalman and brought up a number of questions which had occurred to him as he had read the scriptures. One of the questions was: "How are we to understand that God, the all-knowing, said to Adam, 'Where art thou?'"

"Do you believe," answered the rabbi, "that the Scriptures are eternal and that every era, every generation, and every man is included in them?" The jailer, of course, agreed with the rabbi:

> "Well then," said the rabbi, "in every era God calls to every man: Where are you in the world? So many years and days of those allotted to you have passed, and how far have you gotten in your world?' God says something like this: 'You have lived forty-six years. How far along are you?

> When the chief of the gendarmes [police] heard his age mentioned, he pulled himself together, laid his hand on the rabbi's shoulder and cried: "Bravo!" But his heart trembled.

According to Buber, the chief wanted to try and expose a contradiction in Jewish doctrine. If God knows everything, why did He come to Adam as if inquiring of his whereabouts?

> . . . God seeks Adam, who has hidden himself. He calls into the garden, asking where he is; it would thus seem that he does not

know it, that it is possible to hide from him, and consequently, that he is not all-knowing.

> The rabbi's answer [however] means in effect: "You yourself are Adam, you are the man whom God asks: 'Where art thou?' It would thus seem that the answer gives no explanation of the passage as such. In fact however, it illuminates both the situation of the biblical Adam and that of every man in every time in every place. For, as soon as the chief hears and understands that the biblical question is addressed to him, he is bound to realize what it means when God asks: "Where art thou?" whether the questions be addressed to Adam or to some other man.

In asking this question, Buber goes on to explain that God doesn't expect to learn something He does not know. By asking this question, God intends to produce in us a look inward, to help us to see where we are in our relationship with Him, to see how we are doing in the brief time allotted us in mortality. What He intends to do by asking this question is to produce in Adam, and all of us, an effect which helps us see where we are in facing the responsibilities which He places upon us.

So, what does Adam do? He hides himself to avoid "rendering accounts, to escape responsibility for his way of living."

> . . . Every man hides for this purpose, for every man is Adam and finds himself in Adam's situation. To escape responsibility for his life, he turns existence into a system of hideouts. . . A new situation thus arises, which becomes more and more questionable with every day, with every new hideout. This situation can be precisely defined as follows: Man cannot escape the eye of God, but in trying to hide from him he is hiding from himself. This is the situation into which God's question falls. This question is designed to awaken man and destroy his system of hideouts; it is to show man to what pass he has come and to awake in him the great will to get out of it.

Buber then explained that once God asks the question, the responsibility is then placed squarely on man. It is up to him to become responsible in his relationship with the Almighty.

Whatever success and enjoyment he may achieve, whatever
power he may attain and whatever deeds he may do in this life
will remain [of little consequence], so long as he does not face [up
to God and become responsible for his behavior in mortality and
realize ultimately that he is answerable to God].

As we learn over and over again, the question is not if we will face
tests and trials of life, but when. That being the case, we have to ask
ourselves as might God, our Father, "how are we doing in meeting
these tests of life that come to us?"

GOD IS NOT BEING TESTED, WE ARE

Most people bring into question God's compassion, His love for
His children. We can do what many people do and that is be angry at
the turn of events which "God has forced upon them." Or we can move
ahead, learn from the tragedy or tribulation, and make the most of the
situation in which we find ourselves and glorify God all the while. This
is not to say that this is easy, but it is important to consider how well
we are dealing with the refiner's fire of tribulation. Indeed, Heavenly
Father, in a loving and compassionate way, asks us, from time to time,
how we are doing. He asks over and over again, "Adam, Adam, where
art thou?" In other words, "How are you doing? How are you doing in
facing this burden which is upon you?" Or, how are you doing in your
understanding in my Plan? Do you have faith in the Plan of Salvation
which I have put in place for your benefit? When we consider Heavenly Father asking us such questions, we can take heart, even smile
through our adversity, knowing that He is compassionately blessing us
with this opportunity to grow and develop. Many people, we are sad to
say, usually set up, as Buber suggests, a series of "hideouts" as it were, to
shift the blame for our misery to God—many people in various ways,
"curse God and die" as Job's wife suggested.

These stories and quotes should come as no surprise to anyone. We
are in a mortal condition and can expect tests of all kinds to come our
way— financial tests of all kinds; moral tests—the world is groaning
under the weight of awful sin; physical tests—the health of nations is
not improving around the world—we have to face the threat of cancer,

diabetes, heart disease and all manner of illness; we have to face the fact that there are wars and rumors of wars; earthquakes in divers places, and a ton of other natural disasters that are challenging the world. The list could go on and on. There is no end to it. And there is, therefore, no end to the choices we must make as we pass through the tests. Our choices, the right ones, will make all the difference as Robert Frost tells us in the poem at the beginning of this chapter.

THE GREAT TEST IS TO HAVE FAITH IN THE RESTORED GOSPEL OF JESUS CHRIST

With that said, what is the severe test for a faithful Latter-day Saint who well knows that a loved one who has died is close by in the Spirit World or who is fulfilling his or her part in the great Plan of our Heavenly Father? As I have noted in the beginning of this chapter, the test is to understand and have faith in the Restored Gospel of Jesus Christ. The answer is relatively simple, but it does require faith in the Restoration, in prophets and apostles, in revealed scripture such as the Book of Mormon, the Doctrine and Covenants, and in the Pearl of Great Price along with the Holy Bible.

Although having faith in the Restored Gospel is required to pass the most severe test of life, there are other difficulties that come to us at the passing of a loved one. I will only touch on two of them: loneliness and depression. I want to make it clear, however, that our adherence to the Gospel will help us overcome not only these two particular problems but all of our problems in life, or at least help us cope with them when they come along.

We can prepare right now for the passing of a loved one by continuing to study the Gospel, fully participating in the Church, and in short, doing all that we are commanded and encouraged to do. When we are true and faithful, knowing that a myriad of problems and challenges will come our way, we will be able to deal with the problems in ways which will maximize our learning about the nature of life and death.

THE PAIN OF LONELINESS

Loneliness almost always accompanies the passing of a loved one. Of course, this depends generally on how close the relationship which has been established with a loved one. For the most part, faithful Latter-day Saints develop loving relationships in families, and so when a loved one dies, it can create a great sense of loss, accompanied by loneliness. This is particularly true when a spouse passes on, say after fifty years of marriage. The couple over the course of many years has likely not been separated from one another for any length of time; they become so familiar with one another, with the habits, etc. of the other that when these things are taken away, often times the one left here in mortality simply wanders around missing terribly the one who has passed on. And obviously, even sometimes little things come into play—sleeping alone after sleeping with a spouse for a "lifetime;" dealing with the quiet in a house when there is no one around with whom to talk; and one of the most difficult changes is not being able to discuss ideas, to "talk things over" and to come to joint decisions. Many widows and widowers find these so called "little things" very hard to deal with.

Greg Baer[45] notes,

> "The greatest fear of all for a human being is to be . . . alone."

Those who lose a spouse find it difficult to deal with the night time hours when, in the dark, they are alone where they may dwell on the image and life of the loved one who has passed away.

Many prophets, including of course President Harold B. Lee and many modern-day apostles, have had to deal with loneliness. One ancient prophet who suffered terrible loneliness was Moroni who was alone for a long period of time after the death of his father—his loneliness was painful to him as we read in the Book of Moroni. Not only was he lonely, but he also had to hide out from his enemies who would have killed him had they been able to find him.

> Behold I, Moroni, do finish the record of my father, Mormon. Behold, I have but few things to write, which things I have been commanded by my father.
>
> And now it came to pass that after the great and tremendous battle at Cumorah, behold, the Nephites who had escaped into

---

45   Baer, Greg (2004). Real Love: The truth about finding unconditional love and fulfilling relationships, New York, New York: Penguin Group (USA) Inc. p. 5.

the country southward were hunted by the Lamanites, until they
were all destroyed.

And my father also was killed by them, and I even remain
alone to write the sad tale of the destruction of my people. But behold, they are gone, and I fulfill the commandment of my father.
And whether they will slay me, I know not.

Therefore I will write and hide up the records in the earth;
and whither I go it mattereth not.

Behold, my father hath made this record, and he hath written the intent thereof. And behold, I would write it also if I had
room upon the plates, but I have not; and ore I have none, for I
am alone. My father hath been slain in battle, and all my kinsfolk,
and I have not friends nor wither to go; and how long the Lord
will suffer that I may live I know not (Mormon 8:1-5).

President Lee (as we have read previously in this book) tells us that
Henry Wadsworth Longfellow, the great American poet, grieved for
three years over the loss of his wife. He couldn't function, surely couldn't
write poetry during this period of time. His loneliness had pretty much
rendered him incapable of functioning in a normal way. He was terribly
alone, but as President Lee records, he came out of his loneliness and
despair by coming to the realization that he must press on in his life, that
he wasn't honoring his beloved wife by being dysfunctional.

The most sobering example of loneliness and of particular value
for us is when our Savior hung upon the cross at Calvary. None of us,
however lonely, can match the staggering sense of loneliness the Savior
felt when He was separated from His Father in Heaven. Please catch a
sense of His loneliness in words written by James E. Talmage:[46]

At the ninth hour, or about three in the afternoon, a loud
voice, surpassing the most anguished cry of physical suffering is-
sued from the central cross, rending the dreadful darkness. It was

---

46   Talmage, James E. Jesus the Christ: a study of the Messiah and His Mission according to Holy Scriptures both Ancient and Modern, Salt Lake City, Utah: Deseret Book
Company, p. 613

the voice of the Christ: "Eloi, Eloi, lama sabachthani? which is being interpreted, My God, my God, why has thou forsaken me?" What mind of man can fathom the significance of that awful cry? It seems, that in addition to the fearful suffering incident to crucifixion, the agony of Gethsemane had recurred, intensified beyond human power to endure. In that bitterest hour the dying Christ was alone, alone in most terrible reality. That the supreme sacrifice of the Son might be consummated in all its fullness, the Father seems to have withdrawn the support of His immediate Presence, leaving to the Savior of men the glory of complete victory over the forces of sin and death. The cry from the cross, though heard by all who were near, was understood by few. The first exclamation, Eloi, meaning My God, was misunderstood as a call for Elias.

So loneliness, which was a part of the Savior's suffering, was necessary for the complete victory over the grave; likewise it has an important place in the mourning process for all of us when a loved one passes on. Who doesn't want to be like the Savior, if for a time we're required to be lonely too?

LATTER-DAY SAINTS ARE, IN ONE SENSE, A LONELY PEOPLE; WE ARE WELL ACQUAINTED WITH LONELINESS

Loneliness seems to be the lot, by the way of all Latter-day Saints, by virtue of the fact that we are part of the only true Church on the face of the earth and because of our membership in the Church. We are by nature a "lonely" people. We are partly lonely because we as a people have been invited by the Lord to become a "special" even a "peculiar" people; He has "avouched" us to become so (see Deut. 26:18). And in Deuteronomy 7:6 we read:

> For thou art an holy people unto the Lord thy God: the Lord thy God hath chosen thee to be a special people unto himself, above all people that are upon the face of the earth.

And again from Deuteronomy 14:2 we read,

> For thou art an holy people unto the Lord thy God, and the
> Lord hath chosen thee to be a peculiar people unto himself, above
> all the nations that are upon the earth.

Of course, our peculiarity is defined in a number of ways—we have
a Church structure that is, compared to all other religious structures,
quite peculiar, surely different; and we are peculiar in that we have
apostles and prophets whom we revere and follow; we have scripture,
especially in the form of the Book of Mormon, which is special and
at the very heart of who we are as a people; we have doctrine peculiar
only to us. So by our membership in the Church, we are "alone," in
many ways separated from the rest of the world. President Hinckley
had something to say about this:[47]

> We occupy a special position, you and I. We are members
> of the Church of Jesus Christ of Latter-day Saints. We stand in a
> position of leadership before the world, and there is a loneliness
> in that leadership . . . The crown of the gospel of Jesus Christ
> rests upon our heads. When in this dispensation the Lord declared
> that this is "the only true and living church upon the face of the
> whole earth" (D&C 1:30), we were immediately put in a position
> of loneliness—the loneliness of leadership, from which we can-
> not shrink nor run away. Every true member of this Church who
> lives and breathes the Spirit of the gospel knows something about
> that loneliness. But once having gained a testimony, once know-
> ing that this work is true, we have to live with our conscience. We
> have to live with our faith. We have to live with our testimony. The
> price of adherence to conscience is loneliness. The price of living
> with principle is loneliness.

> The Savior of the world was one who walked alone much of
> the time. I know of no statement more underlined with the pathos
> of loneliness than His statement: "The foxes have holes, and the
> birds of the air have nests; but the Son of man hath not where to
> lay his head" (Matthew 8:20). There is no lonelier picture in all

---

47   The Discourses of President Gordon B. Hinckley, From a speech given in Geneva,
      Switzerland, Volume 1, pages, 523-525.

of history than that of Jesus upon the cross alone, the Redeemer of mankind, the Savior of the world, bringing to pass the Atonement—the Son of God suffering for the sins of mankind. Some of you may have visited the Garden of Gethsemane in Jerusalem. If so, you sensed in your minds the terrible struggle through which He passed there, pleadings with His Father in Heaven, wrestling within Himself until blood came from every pore of His body, and then being led away and nailed to the cross and crying out, "My God, my God, why has thou forsaken me?" (Matthew 27:46).

President Hinckley also explains that Joseph Smith was a man of loneliness. He notes that he was only a young man when he had seen God the Father and His Son Jesus Christ and yet was hated all through his life and terribly persecuted to a point that most of his life he was lonely. President Hinckley said:

> Can you sense something of his loneliness as reflected in these words: "While they were persecuting me, reviling me, and speaking all manner of evil against me falsely for so saying, I was led to say in my heart: Why persecute me for telling the truth? I have actually seen a vision; and who am I that I can withstand God, or why does the world think to make me deny what I have actually seen? For I had seen a vision; I knew it, and I knew that God knew it, and I could not deny it" (Joseph Smith—History 1:25).

I guess we ought to realize that we, at the time of the passing of a loved one, are in good company when lonely, in company with the Savior, with Moroni, and with the Prophet Joseph Smith. It is perfectly natural for us to feel that way. On top of that we, are Latter-day Saints; by virtue of our membership in the Church, we can expect to be all the more lonely. But so be it. Loneliness is part of the test we must pass through our faithfulness to our Savior and Redeemer Jesus Christ.

THE PAIN OF DEPRESSION

Shortly after my wife died, I went to see a doctor for a routine physical checkup. When the doctor learned that my wife had recently died, She asked, "Oh, do you want to live?" I was somewhat surprised at the question, but I was able to answer, "Of course I want to live; I have many family plans and goals, many travel experiences ahead of me, and many other projects I am currently working on." I then asked the doctor, "Why would you ask such a question?" Her response was interesting. She said, "Because some of my patients when they lose a loved one, have often felt that there is nothing to live for!"

Well, if there isn't anything to live for, it's easy to see that depression can set in and become a serious problem for the person in mourning. A faithful Latter-day Saint has much to live for! Much to live for comes from an understanding of the true doctrines which are taught in the Restored Gospel; especially an understanding of the Plan of Salvation and Redemption. The faithful understand that mortality is but a nanosecond in the grand scheme of things; and much of what happens to us eternally depends on what we make of our time in this life. It is true that much of who we are and what we choose in this life may very well rest on many choices we make in the Pre-existence—we accept that—but that doesn't take away from the importance of making wise choices in this life. Indeed, the purpose of mortality, as we have mentioned earlier, is to obtain a physical body, and to see if we are willing to completely obey God's commandments.

Understanding these things may not take away the pain of the passing of a loved one, but it sure helps us to deal with the test of death when it comes along. And some of the tests are severe, even cruel tests that can be discouraging even depressing. Elder Ballard tells a sad and shocking story that shows how easily the pain of depression could set in if one is not rooted clearly and firmly in the Gospel of Jesus Christ:[48]

> Not long after my family and I returned home from our mission in Toronto, one of our young missionary friends appeared at our front door unannounced . He had been an outstanding missionary—one of our very strongest leaders—and now he, too, was home. And he was ready to move on with his life.
>
> "President," he said, "do you remember how you made us all promise that when we met someone we wanted to marry, we'd introduce them to you?"

---

48   Ballard, M. Russell, 1993. Our Search for happiness: An invitation to understand the Church of Jesus Christ of Latter-day Saints, Salt Lake City, Utah: Deseret Book Company, page 75-76.

"Yes," I said, smiling. "I remember that."

"Well," he said with great flourish and obvious delight, "I'd like you to meet my fiancée!"

He introduced us to a wonderful young woman, and we spent a few minutes getting acquainted. It quickly became clear that she was every bit as faithful and strong as he. What a wonderful couple they made—so sweet, so pure, so very much in love. I was honored when they asked me to perform their temple marriage, which was scheduled to take place about three months in the future. We put a circle around that date on the calendar, and then I bade the young couple goodnight.

The next evening I received a telephone call with news that shocked me to the very soul. The young missionary who'd stood in my living room with his fiancée the night before had been killed in an automobile accident. Instead of officiating at his wedding, I was being asked to speak at his funeral.

It is easy to see how people can become depressed when a loved one passes away suddenly as in an accident such as the one described by Elder Ballard. In this case, the young returned missionary was fully faithful in the Church. But there are many Latter-day Saints who are not well grounded in the Gospel; they are the ones that sometimes suffer some degree of depression when a loved one passes away. Sometimes, without an understanding of the doctrines (as I've noted above), especially doctrines pertaining to the Plan of Salvation, eternal life, etc., hearts can become depressed and discouraged about their lives. Obviously, there are many factors that could come into play that would drive depressions and other feelings that often accompany the death of a loved one, particularly the death of a spouse.

In these cases, in addition to seeking professional help, if the depression becomes unmanageable, careful attention to the Gospel and its doctrines can be the very balm needed to recover. Elder Jeffrey R.

Holland and Sister Patricia T. Holland give us good counsel in the following:[49]

> We have been created to become like the Gods. That means we already have inherent within us godly attributes, the greatest of which is Christ-like charity. And the key to emotional health is charity—love. Joy comes from loving and being loved. When this divine attribute is at work in our feelings for our family, our neighbors, our God, and ourselves, we feel joy. When it is immobilized with conflict toward others, toward God, or toward ourselves, we are depressed in our growth and we become depressed in our attitude.

> Depression, conflict, or negativism is often a message to us that we are not growing toward the full measure for which God has created us. Our pain—emotional pain—is a demand that we stop and take time for change in our life because we may be getting off course. As Elder Richard L. Evans used to say, "What's the use of running if you are on the wrong road?" Of course, we all get on the wrong road occasionally; we all have conflicts and discouragements and make mistakes sometimes . . .

Their counsel is very good—we must grow the divine attribute of love, Christ-like charity which is inherent in us. When we do develop the divine attribute of love, our emotional health will improve and we will have the ability to function according to what the Hollands call, the full measure ". . . which God has created in us."

I repeat something I quoted in Chapter Two pertaining to the comprehensive coverage of the atoning sacrifice of the Savior. You will note in this quote that such things as depression, loneliness, sorrow, everything in the human condition is "covered" by the Atonement. Brother Callister says that Jesus Christ took upon himself all sin and transgression:

> . . . the cumulative burden of all depression, all loneliness, all sorrow, all mental, emotional and physical hurt, and all weakness of every kind that afflicts mankind. He knows the depth of

---

49   Holland, Jeffrey R. and Holland, Patricia T. (1989). <u>On Earth as it is in Heaven</u>, Salt Lake City, Utah: Deseret Book Company, page 68.

sorrow that stems from death; he knows the widow's anguish. He understands the agonizing parental pain when children go astray; he has felt the striking pain of cancer, and every other debilitating ailment heaped upon man. Impossible as it may seem, he has somehow taken upon himself those feelings of inadequacy, sometime even utter hopelessness, that accompany our rejections and weaknesses. There is no mortal condition, however gruesome or ugly or hopeless it may seem, that has escaped his grasp or his suffering.[50]

Surely the Savior understands depression, loneliness and every other condition which the human mind can fathom, even the shocking death of a loved one or from a loved one's painful exit from mortality. He urges us, however, to remain true and faithful to our eternal covenants and move forward with faith.

MAIN POINTS DISCUSSED IN CHAPTER FOUR

1. All of us must face, as we sojourn through life, a myriad of challenges which are designed to test us.

2. We learn from the powerful testimony of Job that no matter how difficult the task or test we have to face, it is important that we maintain and develop our testimonies of the Gospel. Said another way, Latter-day Saints must gain a bright and burning testimony of the Restoration and its truthfulness and stand up to the tests of the world which, without doubt are increasing for members of the Church.

3. We learn from Heber C. Kimball's inspired talk that we can't live on borrowed light; we each must develop testimonies to face the tests which will come to all of us.

4. We might consider, as Martin Buber informs us, that we have to avoid making hideouts, that is to say hiding from making an account of our lives to God as we face the challenges and tests of life.

---

50   Callister, Tad R. (2000), <u>The Infinite Atonement</u>, Salt Lake City, Utah: Deseret Book Company, page 104.

5. There is a never-ending list of tests which are put before us in mortality. There doesn't seem to be but more than brief times in our lives when we are not facing one kind of test or another. Tests of mortality come with the territory.

Chapter Five
Our foundation doctrines pertaining to death mostly come from the teachings of the Prophet Joseph Smith

God himself was once as we are now, and is an exalted man, and sits enthroned in yonder heavens! That is the great secret. If the veil were rent today, and the great God who holds this world in its orbit, and who upholds all worlds and all things by His power, was to make himself visible—I say, if you were to see him today, you would see him like a man in form—like yourselves in all the person, image, and very form as a man; for Adam was created in the very fashion, image and likeness of God and received instruction from, and walked, talked and conversed with Him, as one man talks and communes with another.[51]

Joseph Smith, Jr.

In this chapter, I have felt it important to include three funeral speeches delivered by the Prophet Joseph Smith who set forth the most comprehensive doctrines pertaining to life and death and the purpose of life in mortality. In the first speech, readers are treated to some of the most profound doctrines ever uttered in these last days. The Prophet Joseph Smith, at the time he delivered this speech, was under enormous persecution. Even so, he delivered this doctrinally meaningful speech at the passing of his friend Elder King Follett. I have taken the liberty of including only those parts of the speech that provide doctrines related in one way or another to the subject of the dead. There are a few places where the Prophet tangentially talked about other issues; I have taken the liberty of not including them.

---

51   The King Follett Sermon, one of the classics of Church literature, was given by the Prophet Joseph Smith at the April 7, 1844, conference of the Church in Nauvoo, Illinois.

The intent of including the King Follett funeral speech and two others (Patriarch James Adams funeral speech and Judge Higbee funeral speech) is to lay out profound and true doctrines which provide comfort to those who are now mourning the loss of a loved one, or to those who will find themselves mourning sooner or later. The consoling comfort of which I speak can only be found in the doctrines of the Restored Gospel of Jesus Christ as taught in the Church of Jesus Christ of Latter-day Saints. Many of these doctrines are taught powerfully in these speeches. I believe that it is comforting during funerals to have true doctrine explained pertaining to eternal life, the Plan of Salvation and Redemption, and some thoughts pertaining to the Spirit World or the next step on the path to eternal life. It is in these speeches where we find great and comforting doctrine which will help us as we enter a new phase in our lives, after the passing of a loved one.

The subtitles are taken from the speeches as recorded in the Teachings of the Prophet Joseph Smith. I have shifted them from the center of the page to the left margin to preserve the format I have used in this book for side heads.

THE KING FOLLETT FUNERAL SPEECH[52]

delivered by the Prophet Joseph Smith, Jr.

The funeral speech given by the Prophet Joseph Smith on the occasion of the death of Elder King Follett,

April 7, 1844

Beloved Saints: I will call [for] the attention of this congregation while I address you on the subject of the dead. The decease of our

---

52   The King Follett Sermon, one of the classics of Church literature, was given by the Prophet Joseph Smith at the April 7, 1844, conference of the Church in Nauvoo, Illinois. Some twenty thousand Saints were assembled. The Account of the talk noted that it was the funeral sermon for Elder King Follett, a close friend of the Prophet who had been killed in an accident on March 9. Longhand notes of the discourse were made by Willard Richards, Wilford Woodruff, Thomas Bullock, and William Clayton. This reprint was taken from the Documentary History of the Church, vol. 6, pages 302-17.

beloved brother, Elder King Follett, who was crushed in a well by the falling of a tub of rock has more immediately led me to this subject. I have been requested to speak by his friends and relatives but inasmuch as there are a great many in this congregations who live in this city as well as elsewhere, who have lost friends, I feel disposed to speak on the subject in general, and offer you my ideas, so far as I have ability, and so far as I shall be inspired by the Holy Spirit to dwell on this subject.

I want your prayers and faith that I may have the instruction of Almighty God and the gift of the Holy Ghost so that I may set forth things that are true and which can be easily comprehended by you, and that the testimony may carry conviction to your hearts and minds of the truth of what I shall say. Pray that the Lord may strengthen my lungs, stay the winds, and let the prayers of the Saints to heaven appear, that they may enter into the ears of the Lord of Sabaoth, for the effectual prayers of the righteous avail much. There is strength here, and I verily believe that your prayers will be heard.

The Character of God

In the first place, I wish to go back to the beginning—to the morn of creation. There is the starting point for us to look to, in order to understand and be fully acquainted with the mind, purposes and decrees of the Great Elohim, who sits in yonder heavens as he did at the creation of this world. It is necessary for us to have an understanding of God himself in the beginning. If we start right, it is easy to go right all the time; but if we start wrong, we may go wrong, and it be a hard matter to get right.

There are but a very few beings in the world who understand rightly the character of God. The great majority of mankind do not comprehend anything, either that which is past, or that which is to come, as it respects their relationship to God. They do not know, neither do they understand the nature of that relationship; and consequently they know but little above the brute beast, or more than to eat, drink and sleep . . . If a man learns nothing more than to eat, drink and sleep, and does not comprehend any of the designs of God, the beast comprehends the same things.

What Kind of Being Is God?

I want to ask this congregation, every man, woman and child, to answer the question in their own heart, what kind of a being God is? Ask yourselves; turn your thoughts into your hearts, and say if any of you have seen, heard, or communed with him. This is a question that may occupy your attention for a long time. I again repeat the question—What kind of a being is God? Does any man or woman know? Have any of you seen him, heard him, or communed with him? Here is the question that will, peradventure, from this time henceforth occupy your attention. The Scriptures inform us that "This is life eternal that they might know thee, the only true God, and Jesus Christ whom thou has sent."

If any man does not know God, and inquires what kind of a being he is,--if he will search diligently his own heart—if the declaration of Jesus and the apostles be true, he will realize that he has not eternal life; for there can be eternal life on no other principle.

God an Exalted Man

God himself was once as we are now, and is an exalted man, and sits enthroned in yonder heavens! That is the great secret. If the veil were rent today, and the great God who holds this world in its orbit, and who upholds all worlds and all things by His power, was to make himself visible—I say, if you were to see him today, you would see him like a man in form—like yourselves in all the person, image, and very form as a man; for Adam was created in the very fashion, image and likeness of God, and received instruction from, and walked, talked and conversed with Him, as one man talks and communes with another.

In order to understand the subject of the dead, for consolation of those who mourn for the loss of their friends, it is necessary we should understand the character and being of God and how he came to be so; for I am going to tell you how God came to be God. We have imagined and supposed that God was God from all eternity. I will refute that idea, and take away the veil, so that you may see.

These are incomprehensible ideas to some, but they are simple. It is the first principle of the Gospel to know for a certainty the Character of God, and to know that we may converse with him as one man converses with another, and that he was once a man like us; yea, that God himself, the Father of us all, dwelt on an earth, the same as Jesus Christ himself did; and I will show it from the Bible.

Power of the Father and the Son

Here, then, is eternal life—to know the only wise and true God; and you have got to learn how to be Gods yourselves, and to be kings and priests to God, the same as all Gods have done before you, namely, by going from one small degree to another, and from a small capacity to a great one; from grace to grace, from exaltation to exaltation, until you attain to the resurrection of the dead, and are able to dwell in everlasting burnings, and to sit in glory, as do those who sit enthroned in everlasting power. And I want you to know that God, in the last days, while certain individuals are proclaiming his name, is not trifling with you or me.

The Righteous to Dwell in Everlasting Burnings

These are the first principles of consolation. How consoling to be mourners when they are called to part with a husband, wife, father, mother, child, or dear relative, to know that, although the earthly tabernacle is laid down and dissolved, they shall rise again to dwell in everlasting burnings in immortal glory, not to sorrow, suffer, or die any more, but they shall be heirs of God and joint heirs with Jesus Christ. What is it? To inherit the same power, the same glory and the same exaltation, until you arrive at the station of a God, and ascend the throne of eternal power, the same as those who have gone before. What did Jesus do? Why; I do the things I saw my Father do when worlds came rolling into existence. My Father worked out his kingdom with fear and trembling, and I must do the same; and when I get my kingdom, I shall present it to my Father, so that he may obtain kingdom upon kingdom, and it will exalt him in glory. He will then take a higher exaltation, and I will take his place, and thereby become exalted myself. So that Jesus treads in the tracks of his Father, and inherits what God did before; and God is thus glorified and exalted in the salvation and exaltation of all his children. It is plain beyond disputation, and you thus learn some of the first principles of the Gospel, about which so much hath been said.

When you climb up a ladder, you must begin at the bottom, and ascend step by step, until you arrive at the top; and so it is with the principles of the Gospel—you must begin with the first, and go on until you learn all the principles of exaltation. But it will be a great while after you have passed through the veil before you will have learned them. It is not all to be comprehended in this world; it will be a great work to learn our salvation and exaltation even beyond the grave.

Meaning of the Hebrew Scriptures

I shall comment on the very first Hebrew word in the Bible: I will make a comment on the very first sentence of the history of creation in the Bible—Berosheit. I want to analyze the word. Baith—in, by, through, and everything else. Rosh—the head. Sheit—grammatical termination. When the inspired man wrote it, he did not put the baith there. An old Jew without any authority added the word; he thought it too bad to begin to talk about the head! It read first, "The head one of the Gods brought forth the Gods." That is the true meaning of the words, Baurau signifies to bring forth . . . Thus the head God brought forth the Gods in the grand council.

. . . The head God called together the Gods and sat in grand council to bring forth the world. The grand councilors sat at the head in yonder heavens and contemplated the creation of the worlds which were created at the time.

A Council of the Gods

In the beginning, the head of the Gods called a council of the Gods; and they came together and concocted a plan to create the world and people it. When we begin to learn this way, we begin to learn the only true God, and what kind of a being we have got to worship. Having a knowledge of God, we begin to know how to approach him, and how to ask so as to receive an answer. When we understand the character of God, and know how to come to him, he begins to unfold the heavens to us, and to tell us all about it. When we are ready to come to him, he is ready to come to us.

Now, I ask all who hear me, why the learned men who are preaching salvation, say that God created the heavens and the earth out of nothing? The reason is that they are unlearned in the things of God, and have not the gift of the Holy Ghost; they account it blasphemy in any one to contradict their idea. If you tell them that God made the world out of something, they will call you a fool.

Meaning of the Word Create

. . . the word create came from the word "baurau" which does not mean to create out of nothing; it means to organize; the same as a man would organize materials and build a ship. Hence, we infer that God had materials to organize the world out of chaos—chaotic matter, which is element, and in which dwells all the glory. Element had an existence from the time he had. The pure principles of element are principles which can never be destroyed; they may be organized and re-organized, but not destroyed. They had no beginning, and can have no end.

The Immortal Spirit

I have another subject to dwell upon, which is calculated to exalt man; but it is impossible for me to say much on this subject. I shall therefore just touch upon it, for time will not permit me to say all. It is associated with the subject of the resurrection of the dead—namely, the soul—the mind of man—the immortal spirit. Where did we come from? . . . God made a tabernacle and put a spirit into it, and it became a living soul. . . . God made man out of the earth and put into him Adam's spirit, and so became a living body.

The mind or the intelligence which man possesses is coequal with God himself. I know that my testimony is true; hence, when I talk to these mourners, what have they lost? Their relatives and friends are only separated from their bodies for a short season; their spirits which existed with God have left the tabernacle of clay only for a little moment, as it were; and they now exist in a place where they converse together the same as we do on the earth.

I am dwelling on the immortality of the spirit of man. Is it logical to say that the intelligence of spirits is immortal, and yet that it had a beginning? The intelligence of spirits had no beginning, neither will it have an end. That is good logic. That which has a beginning may have an end. There never was a time when there were not spirits; for they are co-equal [co-eternal] with our Father in heaven.

I want to reason more on the spirit of man; for I am dwelling on the body and spirit of man—on the subject of the dead. I take my ring from my finger and liken it unto the mind of man—the immortal part, because it has no beginning. Suppose you cut it in two; then it has a beginning and an end; but join it again, and it continues on eternal round. So with the spirit of man. As the Lord liveth, if it had a beginning, it will have an end . . . God never had the power to create the spirit of man at all, God himself could not create himself.

The Power to Advance in Knowledge

The first principles of man are self-existent with God. God himself, finding he was in the midst of spirits and glory, because he was more intelligent, saw proper to institute laws whereby the rest could have a privilege to advance like himself. The relationship we have with God places us in a situation to advance in knowledge. He has power to institute laws to instruct the weaker intelligences, that they may be exalted with himself, so that they might have one glory upon another, and all that knowledge, power, glory, and intelligence, which is requisite in order to save them in the world of spirits.

This is good doctrine. It tastes good. I can taste the principles of eternal life, and so can you.

The Relation of Man to God

I want to talk more of the relation of man to God. I will open your eyes in relation to your dead . . . Hence the responsibility, the awful responsibility, that rests upon us in relation to our dead; for all the spirits who have not obeyed the Gospel in the flesh must either obey it in the spirit or be damned. Solemn thought!—dreadful thought! Is there nothing to be done?—no preparation—no salvation for our fathers and friends who have died without having had the opportunity to obey the decrees of the Son of Man?

Our Greatest Responsibility

What promises are made in relation to the subject of the salvation of the dead? And what kind of characters are those who can be saved, although their bodies are moldering and decaying in the grave? When his commandments teach us, it is in view of eternity; for we are looked upon by God as though we were in eternity. God dwells in eternity, and does not view things as we do.

The greatest responsibility in this world that God has laid upon us is to seek after our dead. The Apostle says, "They without us cannot be made perfect" (Hebrews 11:40) for it is necessary that the sealing power should be in our hands to seal our children and our dead for the fullness of the dispensation of times—a dispensation to meet the promises made by Jesus Christ before the foundation of the world for the salvation of man.

The Unpardonable Sin

. . . If a man has knowledge, he can be saved; although if he has been guilty of great sins, he will be punished for them. But when he consents to obey the Gospel whether here or in the world of spirits, he is saved.

. . . the salvation of Jesus Christ was wrought out for all men, in order to triumph over the devil; for if it did not catch him in one place, it would in another, for he stood up as a Savior. All will suffer until they obey Christ himself.

All sins shall be forgiven, except the sin against the Holy Ghost; for Jesus will save all except the sons of perdition. What must a man do to commit the unpardonable sin? He must receive the Holy Ghost, have the heavens opened unto him, and know God, and then sin against Him. After a man has sinned against the Holy Ghost, there is no repentance for him.

"In My Father's House"

The best men bring forth the best works. The man who tells you words of life is the man who can save you.

. . . Jesus said, "In my Father's house are many mansions; if it were not so, I would have told you. I go to prepare a place for you" (John 14:2). Paul says, "There is one glory of the sun, and another glory of the moon, and another glory of the stars; for one star differeth from another star in glory, have we to console us in relation to the dead? We have reason to have the greatest hope and consolations for our dead of any people on the earth; for we have seen them walk worthily in our midst, and seen them sink asleep in the arms of Jesus; and those who have died in the faith are now [destined to be] in the celestial kingdom of God.

Righteous Mourners Rejoice

You mourners have occasion to rejoice, speaking of the death of Elder King Follett; for your husband and father is gone to wait until the resurrection of the dead—until the perfection of the remainder; for at the resurrection your friend will rise in perfect felicity and go to celestial glory, while many must wait myriads of years before they can receive the like blessings; and your expectations and hopes are far above what man can conceive; for why has God revealed it to us?

I am authorized to say, by the authority of the Holy Ghost, that you have no occasion to fear; for he is gone to the home of the just. Don't mourn, don't weep. I know it by the testimony of the Holy Ghost that is within me; and you may wait for your friends to come forth to meet you in the morn of the celestial world.

Rejoice, O Israel! Your friends who have been murdered for the truth's sake in the persecutions shall triumph gloriously in the celestial world, while their murderers shall welter for ages in torment, even until they shall have paid the uttermost farthing.

I have a father, brothers, children, and friends who have gone to a world of spirits. They are only absent for a moment. They are in the spirit, and we shall soon meet again. The time will soon arrive when the trumpet shall sound. When we depart, we shall hail our mothers, fathers, friends, and all whom we love, who have fallen asleep in Jesus. There will be no fear of mobs, persecutions, or malicious lawsuits and arrests; but it will be an eternity of felicity.

Baptism

I will leave this subject here, and make a few remarks on the subject of baptism. The baptism of water, without the baptism of fire and the Holy Ghost attending it, is of no use; they are necessarily and inseparably connected. An individual must be born of water and the Spirit in order to get into the kingdom of God.

There is one God, one Father, one Jesus, one hope of our calling, one baptism. Many talk of baptism not being essential to salvation; but this kind of teaching would lay the foundation of their damnation.

A Call to Repentance

Hear it, all ye ends of the earth—all ye priests, all ye sinners, and all men. Repent! Repent! Obey the Gospel. Turn to God; for your religion won't save you, and you will be damned.

I have intended my remarks for all, both rich and poor, bond and free, great and small. I have no enmity against any man. I love you all; but I hate some of your deeds. I am your best friend . . .

. . . I don't blame anyone for not believing my history. If I had not experienced what I have, I could not have believed it myself. I never did harm any man since I was born in the world. My voice is always for peace.

I cannot lie down until all my work is finished. I never think any evil, nor do anything to the harm of my fellow-man. When I am called by the trump of the archangel and weighed in the balance, you will all know me then. I add no more. God bless you all. Amen.

THE PATRIARCH JAMES ADAMS FUNERAL SPEECH[53]

delivered by the Prophet Joseph Smith, Jr.

This is the second funeral speech included here from which we can find great comfort. The Prophet Joseph gave this speech to obviously comfort the family of Patriarch James Adams, but to also give the Saints powerful doctrine pertaining to the great Plan of Salvation. Throughout these funeral speeches, the Prophet emphasizes the blessing and privilege we as Latter-day Saints enjoy of having revelation

---

53 Teachings of the Prophet Joseph Smith, (selected and arranged by Joseph Smith, Salt Lake City, Utah: Deseret Book Company; pages 324-326. See also the. Documentary History of the Church, 6:50-52

which confirms the truth of all things and is so comforting to those who are mourning at the passing of a loved one.

Excerpts from Remarks given by the Prophet Joseph Smith on the Demise of Patriarch James Adams

October 9, 1843
How Salvation Is Acquired

All men know that they must die. And it is important that we should understand the reasons and causes of our exposure to the vicissitudes of life and of death, and the designs and purposes of God in our coming into the world, our sufferings here, and our departure hence. What is the object of our coming into existence, then dying and falling away, to be here no more? It is but reasonable to suppose that God would reveal something in reference to the matter, and it is a subject we ought to study more than any other. We ought to study it day and night, for the world is ignorant in reference to their true condition and relation. If we have any claim on our Heavenly Father for anything, it is for knowledge on this important subject. Could we read and comprehend all that has been written from the days of Adam, on the relation of man to God and angels in a future state, we should know very little about it. Reading the experience of others, or the revelation given to them, can never give us a comprehensive view of our condition and true relation to God. Knowledge of these things can only be obtained by experience through the ordinances of God set forth for this purpose. Could you gaze into heaven five minutes, you would know more than you would by reading all that ever was written on the subject.

We are only capable of comprehending that certain things exist, which we may acquire by certain fixed principles. If men would acquire salvation, they have got to be subject, before they leave this world, to certain rules and principles, which were fixed by an unalterable decree before the world was.

The disappointments of hopes and expectations at the resurrection would be indescribably dreadful.

Angels and Spirits

The organization of the spiritual and heavenly worlds, and of spiritual and heavenly beings, was agreeable to the most perfect order and harmony; their limits and bounds were fixed irrevocably, and voluntarily subscribed to in their heavenly estate by themselves, and were by our first parents subscribed to upon the earth. Hence, the importance of embracing and subscribing to principles of eternal truth by all men upon the earth that expect eternal life.

I assure the Saints that truth, in reference to these matters, can and may be known through the revelations of God in the way of His ordinances, and in answer to prayer . . .

Spirits can only be revealed in flaming fire and glory. Angels have advanced further, their light and glory being tabernacle; and hence they appear in bodily shape. The spirits of just men are made ministering servants to those who are sealed unto life eternal, and it is through them that the sealing power comes down.

Patriarch Adams is now one of the spirits of the just men made perfect; and, if revealed now, must be revealed in fire; and the glory could not be endured. Jesus showed Himself to His disciples, and they thought it was His spirit, and they were afraid to approach His spirit. Angels have advanced higher in knowledge and power than spirits.

Concerning Brother James Adams, it should appear strange that so good and so great a man was hated. The deceased ought never to have had an enemy. But so it was. Wherever light shone, it stirred up darkness. Truth and error, good and evil cannot be reconciled. Judge Adams had some enemies, but such a man ought not to have had one. I saw him first at Springfield, when on my way from Missouri to Washington. He sought me out when a stranger, took me to his home, encouraged and cheered me, and gave me money. He has been a most intimate friend. I anointed him to the patriarchal power—to receive the keys of knowledge and power, by revelation to himself. He has had revelations concerning his departure and has gone to a more important work. When men are prepared, they are better off to go hence. Brother Adams has gone to open up a more effectual door for the dead. The spirits of the just are exalted to a greater and more glorious work; hence they are blessed in their departure to the world of spirits. Enveloped in flaming fire, they are not far from us, and know and understand our thoughts, feelings and motions, and are often pained therewith.

Flesh and blood cannot go there; but flesh and bones, quickened by the Spirit of God can.

If we would be sober and watch in fasting and prayer, God would turn away sickness from our midst.

Hasten the work in the Temple, renew your exertions to forward all the work of the last days, and walk before the Lord in soberness and righteousness. Let the Elders and Saints do away with light minded-ness, and be sober.

THE JUDGE HIGBEE FUNERAL SPEECH[54]
delivered by the Prophet Joseph Smith

This is the third funeral address I want to include here given by the Prophet which should be inspiring to us all. In his always powerful but somewhat different way, he bears witness of the Plan of Salvation which God has put in place through the blessing of the Holy Ghost who reveals all things.

We should note that this speech and others the Prophet gave were recorded by scribes who would likely compare notes and come to some sort of consensus but there would, undoubtedly be something not completely accurate. Be that as it may, the doctrine is powerful and very comforting to all of us who are mourning the passing of a loved one.

Excerpts from remarks given by Joseph Smith the Prophet on the occasion of the funeral of Judge Higbee

August 13, 1843

Brethren and Sisters, you will find these words in II Peter 3:10-11—"But the day of the Lord will come as a thief in the night; in the which the heavens shall pass away with a great noise, and the elements

---

54   Teachings of the Prophet Joseph Smith, (selected and arranged by Joseph Smith, Salt Lake City, Utah: Deseret Book Company; pages 324-326. See also the. Documentary History of the Church, 6:50-52

shall melt with fervent heat, the earth also and the works that are therein shall be burned up."

See then that all these things shall be dissolved, what manner of persons ought ye to be in all holy conversation and godliness."

The great thing for us to know is to comprehend what God did institute before the foundation of the world. Who knows it? It is the constitutional disposition of mankind to set up stakes and set bounds to the works and ways of the Almighty.

But I will give you a more painful thought. Suppose you have an idea of a resurrection, etc., and yet know nothing at all of the Gospel, nor comprehend one principle of the order of heaven, but find yourselves disappointed—yes, at last find yourselves disappointed in every hope or anticipation, when the decision goes forth from the lips of the Almighty. Would not this be a greater disappointment—a more painful thought than annihilation?

Where has Judge Higbee gone?

Covenants of the Fathers Revealed

Who is there that would not give all his goods to feed the poor, and pour out his gold and silver to the four winds, to go where Judge Higbee has gone?

That which hath been hid from before the foundation of the world is revealed to babes and sucklings in the last days.

The world is reserved unto burning in the last days. He shall send Elijah the prophet, and he shall reveal the covenants of the fathers in relation to the children, and the covenants of the children in relation to the fathers.

Four destroying angels holding power over the four quarters of the earth until the servants of God are sealed in their foreheads, which signifies sealing the blessing upon their heads, meaning the everlasting covenant, thereby making their calling and election sure. When a seal is put upon the father and mother, it secures their posterity, so that they cannot be lost, but will be saved by virtue of the covenant of their father and mother.

To the mourners I would say—Do as the husband and father would instruct you, and you shall be reunited.

Note: The scribes then made these additions:

The speaker continued to teach the doctrine of election and the sealing powers and principles, and spoke of the doctrine of election with the seed of Abraham, and the sealing of blessings upon his posterity, and the sealing of the fathers and children, according to the declarations of the prophets. He then spoke of Judge Higbee in the world of spirits, and the blessing which he would obtain, and of the kind spirit and disposition of Judge Higbee while living; none of which was reported (see Documentary History of the Church, 5:529-531)

MAIN POINTS DISCUSSED
IN CHAPTER FIVE

1. The great majority of people do not comprehend the character of God. In order to understand the subject of the dead, for consolation of those who mourn for the loss of their friends, it is necessary we should understand the character and being of God

2. We must know God, the only true God, and Jesus Christ in order to enjoy eternal life.

3. God Himself was once as we are now and is an exalted man—He has form like a man.

4. We must learn to become god's ourselves—learning, progressing eventually to sit on thrones in everlasting power.

5. Jesus treads in the path of His Father—Jesus takes His Father's place as the Father progresses.

6. Having a correct knowledge of the character of God, we know how to approach Him—the right questions to ask Him.

7. God had materials to organize the world; these materials have always existed—they have no end.

8. God made man out of the earth and "breathed" life into him.

9. Man's intelligence has no beginning and has no end.

10. God never had the power to create the spirit of man; God also could not create Himself.

11. The greatest responsibility in this world that God has laid upon us is to seek after our dead.

12. When men consent to obey the Gospel whether here or in the world of spirits, he is saved.

13. All sins shall be forgiven, except the sin against the Holy Ghost.

14. There is in the eternal worlds, a glory of the sun; a glory of the moon; and a glory of the stars.

15. Those who die in the faith are destined to be in the celestial kingdom of God.

16. People who die go to the Spirit World to await the resurrection.

17. When a faithful person dies, there is no need to mourn, to fear, or to weep; they await us on the other side of the veil.

18. There is one God, one Father, one Jesus, one hope of our calling, one baptism.

19. All of us must repent in order to be saved.

20. When the Lord returns to the earth, He will come as a thief in the night.

21. God has revealed much to the children of men pertaining to life after death.

22. If men would acquire salvation, they have got to be subject, before they leave this world, to certain rules and principles which were fixed by an unalterable decree before the world was.

23. The truth of God's workings on earth can only be comprehended by revelation.

24. When men are prepared, they are better off on the other side of the veil.

Chapter Six
Our great "March of Progress" includes especially the preaching of the gospel

But behold, from among the righteous, he organized his forces and appointed messengers, clothed with power and authority, and commissioned them to go forth and carry the light of the gospel to them that were in darkness, even to all the spirits of men; and thus was the gospel preached to the dead

And the chosen messengers went forth to declare the acceptable day of the Lord and proclaim liberty to the captives who were bound, even unto all who would repent of their sins and receive the gospel.

Doctrine and Covenants 138:30-31

OUR LOSS IS THEIR GAIN

There is much comfort to be had in the many pronouncements of living prophets pertaining to the death of loved ones. Of course we mourn and sorrow over the loss of loved ones; it's appropriate that we do so. We sense the loss but, as Francis M. Lyman once said, "our loss is their gain." By "their" he means those who have waited on the other side of the veil for the one who may have died.

> . . . for it is our loss; but is their gain, for it is in the march of progress, advancement and development.[55]

This is a very nice sentiment to be sure. We miss terribly a loved one who has passed on but the rejoicing of loved ones on the other side of the veil must be taken into consideration also—it is our loss (for a time) but it is also the gain of those who greet our loved one. We have

---

55   Lyman, Francis M., <u>Conference Report</u>, October 1909, 18-19.

to remember that those on the other side of the veil are very happy to greet those who pass away and move on to the world of spirits.

I want to say here that even though we use the word "loss," we actually never "lose" a loved one when he or she dies; no one ever gets lost. In and of itself, this is a wonderful doctrine—we'll always be cared for as we progress to the other side of the veil. We use the word "loss" as a part of our language when someone passes away. But as I've said above we only are separated for a time; our loved ones have only passed through the veil and at some later date, sooner or later, we will join the loved one and continue our progression along with them in that realm of the spirits. In that sense we really never "lose" a loved one.

So even though we use the word "lose" as in the case of President Lee's statement, we are only talking about losing someone for a short time while we remain in mortality; we surely don't "lose" them forever.

PREACHING THE GOSPEL WILL OCCUPY MOST OF OUR TIME

And so when people die, they march into the eternities, into the world of spirits. And what awaits them is a very active lifestyle; they are very busy. And while they're busy, they never get tired, or bored, or disinterested; they are excited and highly motivated in the work they are doing.

So what do people do on the other side of the veil? Well, for starters, we are told that they are busily engaged in doing missionary work, preaching the Gospel to those who are unacquainted with it in the Spirit World. It's the kind of work we would love to do full time in mortality; but alas, we have to make a living. In truth, it is basically the only work that will be going on in the world of spirits; actually, when you think about it, what else is there of more importance? Our deceased loved ones are preaching the Gospel hoping, I suppose, that we are doing temple work for those who accept the truth.

President Wilford Woodruff gives us great insight about the other side of the veil and the work that is going on there. He says:

> I feel at liberty to reveal to this assembly this morning what has
> been revealed to me since we were here yesterday morning. If the

veil could be taken from our eyes and we could see into the spirit world, we would see that Joseph Smith, Brigham Young and John Taylor had gathered together every spirit that ever dwelt in the flesh in this Church since its organization. We would also see the faithful apostles and elders of the Nephites who dwelt in the flesh in the days of Jesus Christ. In that assembly we would also see Isaiah and every prophet and apostle that ever prophesied of the great work of God. In the midst of these spirits we would see the Son of God, the Savior, who presides and guides and controls the preparing of the kingdom of God on the earth and in heaven. From that body of spirits, when we shout "Hosannah to God and the Lamb!" there is a mighty shout goes up of "Glory to God in the Highest!" that the God of Israel has permitted his people to finish this temple and pre-pare it for the great work that lies before the Latter-day Saints. These patriarchs and prophets who have wished for this day, rejoice in the spirit world that the day has come when the saints of the Most High God have had power to carry out this great mission.[56]

President Woodruff[57] noted that in the work of the ministry in the spirit world, everyone who has died in the faith, all Priesthood leaders—everyone—as soon as they pass through the veil will be about preaching the Gospel to the legions of people who have died without a knowledge of the Restored Gospel. In other words, people who have passed through the veil will have plenty of work to do.   In a discourse given at the funeral of Mary A. Freeze, President Joseph F. Smith said that those who have died and who have been true and faithful to their covenants are preaching the gospel in the world of spirits to those who have died without having the privilege of hearing the gospel in mortal-ity. He reiterated a statement made by the Prophet Joseph Smith who proclaimed that we cannot be perfect without them and they cannot be perfect without us, hence the serious preaching of the Gospel.

He went on with a wonderful insight about women preaching the Gospel in the spirit world. From <u>Gospel Doctrine</u>, we read:

> Now, among all these millions of spirits that have lived on the earth and have passed away, from generation to generation, since

---

56   Woodruff, Wilford, <u>A Book of Remembrance</u>, 81-82.
57   Woodruff, Wilford, <u>Journal of Discourses</u>, 22:334.

the beginning of the world, without knowledge of the gospel—
among them you may count that at least one-half are women.
Who is going to preach the gospel to the women? Who is going
to carry the testimony of Jesus Christ to the hearts of the women
who have passed away without a knowledge of the gospel? Well, to
my mind it is a simple thing. These good sisters who have been set
apart, ordained to the work, called to it, authorized by the authority of the Holy Priesthood to minister for their sex, in the House
of God for the living and for the dead, will be fully authorized and
empowered to preach the gospel and minister to the women while
the elders and prophets are preaching it to the men . . . Those who
are authorized to preach the gospel here and are appointed here
to do that work will not be idle after they have passed away, but
will continue to exercise the rights that they obtain here under the
Priesthood of the Son of God to minister for the salvation of those
who have died without a knowledge of the truth.[58]

President Joseph F. Smith had a most remarkable vision on October 3, 1918 in which he saw the Savior, while His body lay in the
tomb, visit the spirits in prison. This vision is reported in Doctrine and
Covenants 138. Among other things the scripture makes very clear that
the Savior visited a "vast multitude" who were:

> "rejoicing in the hour of their deliverance from the chains of
> death" (verse 18).

> And there he preached to them the everlasting gospel, the
> doctrine of the resurrection and the redemption of mankind from
> the fall, and from individual sins on conditions of repentance
> (verse 19).

The Savior did not go to the wicked in the spirit world but instead,

> . . . from among the righteous, he organized his forces and ap-
> pointed messengers, clothed with power and authority, and com-
> missioned them to go forth and carry the light of the gospel to

---

58   Smith, Joseph F. (1919) <u>Gospel Doctrine: Selections from the Sermons and Writings</u>
<u>of Joseph F. Smith</u>: Deseret Book Company, pages 460-461

them that were in darkness, even to all the spirits of men; and thus was the gospel preached to the dead (verse 30).

> And the chosen messengers went forth to declare the acceptable day of the Lord and proclaim liberty to the captives who were bound, even unto all who would repent of their sins and receive the gospel (verse 31).

From this remarkable vision, we learn a number of very important fundamental principles of the Gospel. We learn of the reality of the Savior's resurrection; of His concern for the souls of all of Heavenly Father's children; of His desire that all men hear His Gospel; of His organizing His righteous messengers; and of the proclaiming of the Gospel message to all of the spirits in the spirit world.

Orson Pratt confirms the idea that the Savior was actively engaged in visiting the people in the world of spirits even while His body lay in the tomb. He says:

> Jesus himself set the example and pattern for others. While his body lay in the silent tomb, his noble spirit was not idle; hence, Peter says, that Jesus, being put to death in the flesh, was quickened by the Spirit, by which also he went and preached to the spirits in prison that were sometime disobedient in the days of Noah, etc. . . . Those antediluvian spirits had suffered in the prison some two thousand years, and upwards; they needed some information, and Jesus went to enlighten them.[59]

From these various thoughts expressed in scripture and through utterances of apostles and prophets, we know for sure that those of our loved ones who have died and passed to the other side of the veil are engaged in a marvelous work, it is part of their march of progress.

From Parley P. Pratt,[60] we learn of the condition of people in the world of spirits. He says:

> In the world of spirits there are apostles, prophets, elders, and members of the Church of the saints, holding keys of priesthood,

---

59   Pratt, Orson, Journal of Discourses 2:371).
60   Pratt, Parley P. (1965) Key to Theology, Salt Lake City, Utah: Deseret Book Company, pages 128-129.

and power to teach, comfort, instruct, and proclaim the gospel to their fellow spirits, after the pattern of Jesus Christ.

In the same world there are also the spirits of Catholics and Protestants of every sect, who have all need to be taught and to come to the knowledge of the true unchangeable gospel in its fullness and simplicity, that they may be judged the same as if they had been privileged with the same in the flesh.

There is also the Jew, the [Mahomeran], the infidel, who did not believe in Christ while in the flesh. All these must be taught, must come to the knowledge of the crucified and risen Redeemer, and hear the glad tidings of the gospel.

There are also all the varieties of the heathen spirits; the noble and refined philosopher, poet, patriot or statesmen of Rome or Greece, the enlightened Socrates and Plato, and their like, together with every grade of spirits down to the most uncultivated of the savage world.

All these must be taught, enlightened, and must bow the knee to the eternal King, for the decree hath gone forth that unto him every knee shall bow and every tongue confess.

O, what a field of labor, of benevolence, of missionary enterprise now opens to the apostles and elders of the Church of the saints! As this field opens they will begin to realize more fully the extent of their divine mission, and the meaning of the great command to "preach the gospel to every creature."

In this vast field of labor the priesthood are, in a great measure, occupied during their sojourn in the world of spirits, while awaiting the resurrection of the body, and at the same time they themselves are edified, improved and greatly advanced and matured in the science of divine theology.

It seems quite clear that the main responsibility for faithful Latter-day Saints when they arrive in the world of spirits is to preach the Gospel to everyone. In Heavenly Father's great love and mercy, all of

His children must be given an opportunity to hear the truth, weigh it, and hopefully accept it. From the sounds of things, our loved ones who have passed through the veil to the other side will be very busy preaching the Gospel. It also appears that they will have far greater success in preaching the gospel there than they may have enjoyed here in mortality. In the words of Lorenzo Snow,[61]

> The circumstances there will be a thousand times more favorable.

And the interesting thing to remember is that there won't be Satan there to encumber the work. According to President Brigham Young, those who do go to the other side will have the same Priesthood power as they had while in mortality but that they will have power over the evil one; they won't be disturbed or harmed in anyway by Satan.[62]

Although the next quote is very long, it is powerful in that it gives us a glimpse into the spirit world as seen through the eyes of Jedediah M. Grant who told of his experience to Heber C. Kimball who, in turn, told the story at Brother Grant's funeral.[63]

> I went to see him [Jedediah M. Grant] one day last week, and he reached out his hand and shook hands with me; he could not speak, but he shook hands warmly with me. . . . I laid my hands upon him and blessed him, and asked God to strengthen his lungs that he might be easier, and in two or three minutes he raised himself up and talked for about an hour as busily as he could, telling me what he had seen and what he understood, until I was afraid he would weary himself, when I arose and left him.
>
> He said to me, "Brother Heber, I have been into the spirit world two nights in succession, and, of all the dreads that ever came across me, the worst was to have to again return to my body, though I had to do it. But O," says he, "the order and government that were there! When in the spirit world, I saw the order of righteous men and women; beheld them organized in their several grades, and there appeared to be no obstruction to my vision; I

61   Snow, Lorenzo, Millennial Star 56:50.
62   Young, Brigham, Journal of Discourses 3:371
63   Heber C. Kimball, Funeral of Jedediah M. Grant, Dec. 4, 1856.

could see every man and woman in their grade and order. I looked to see whether there was any disorder there, but there was none; neither could I see any death nor any darkness, disorder or confusion." He said that the people he there saw were organized in family capacities; and when he looked at them he saw grade after grade and all were organized and in perfect harmony. He would mention one item after another and say, "Why, it is just as Brother Brigham says it is; it is just as he told us many a time."

That is a testimony as to the truth of what Brother Brigham teaches us, and I know it is true, from what little light I have.

He saw the righteous gathered together in the spirit world, there and were no wicked spirits among them. He saw his wife; she was the first person that came to him. He saw many that he knew, but did not have conversation with any except his wife, Caroline. She came to him, and he said that she looked beautiful and had their little child, that died on the plains, in her arms, and said, "Mr. Grant, here is little Margaret; you know that the wolves ate her up, but it did not hurt her; here she is all right."

To my astonishment," he said, "when I looked at families there was a deficiency in some, there was a lack, for I saw families that would not be permitted to come and dwell together, because they had not honored their calling here."

He asked his wife, Caroline, where Joseph and Hyrum and Father Smith and others were, she replied, "they have gone away ahead to perform and transact business for us." The same as when Brother Brigham and his brethren left Winter Quarters and came here to search out a home; they came to find a location for their brethren.

He also spoke of the buildings he saw there, remarking that the Lord gave Solomon wisdom and poured gold and silver into his hands that he might display his skill and ability, and said that the temple erected by Solomon was much inferior to the most ordinary buildings he saw in the spirit world.

"In regard to gardens," says Brother Grant, "I have seen good gardens on this earth, but I never saw any to compare with those that were there. I saw flowers of numerous kinds, and some with from fifty to a hundred different colored flowers growing upon one stalk." We have many kinds of flowers on the earth, and I suppose those very articles came from heaven, or they would not be here.

After mentioning the things that he had seen, he spoke how much he disliked to return and resume his body, after having seen the beauty and glory of the spirit world, where the righteous spirits are gathered together.

Some may marvel at my speaking about these things, for many profess to believe that we have no spiritual existence. But do you not believe that my spirit was organized before it came to my body here? And do you not think there can be houses and gardens, fruit trees, and every other good thing there? The spirits of those things were made, as well as our spirits, and it follows that they can exist upon the same principle.

After speaking of the gardens and the beauty of everything there, Brother Grant said that he felt extremely sorrowful at having to leave so beautiful a place and come back to earth, for he looked upon his body with loathing, but was obliged to enter it again.

He said that after he came back he could look upon his family and see the spirit that was in them; and the darkness that was in them; and that he conversed with them about the gospel, and what they should do, and they replied, "Well, Brother Grant, perhaps it is so, and perhaps it is not." And said that was the state of this people, to a great extent, for many are full of darkness and will not believe me.

I never had a view of the righteous assembling in the spirit world, but I have had a view of the hosts of hell, and have seen them as plainly as I see you today. The righteous spirits gather together to prepare and qualify themselves for a future day, and evil spirits have no power over them, though they are constantly striving for the mastery. I have seen evil spirits attempt to overcome those holding the priesthood, and I know how they act.

Such is the opportunity for all of us; we will have the privilege of working to build the Kingdom of God on the other side of the veil in company with those we love. It is part of the "march of progress" which allows us and those we teach to continue to polish and refine our lives so that we are in complete harmony with the will of our Heavenly Father. In this life, we want to have the assurance that the "course of life [we] pursue is according to the will of God . . ."[64] In the coming life, we will want the same assurance—this is the "march of progress."

MAIN POINTS DISCUSSED IN CHAPTER SIX

1. From every indication, people on the other side of the veil are very busy and yet are never tired, bored, or disinterested in what they are doing.

2. The main responsibility which will be given to those on the other side of the veil is to preach the Gospel.

3. All of God's children must be given an opportunity to hear the Gospel of Jesus Christ.

4. When preaching the Gospel in the spirit world, we will enjoy much more success than we enjoy in mortality.

5. All of God's children in the spirit world yearn for, and are anxious for, the time when they will be resurrected.

6. In this life, we want to be sure we are progressing and growing in the Gospel; in the next we will continue this "march of progress" as well.

---

64   Smith, Joseph, <u>Lectures on Faith delivered to the School of the Prophets in Kirtland, Ohio 1834-35.</u> Salt Lake City, Utah: Deseret Book Company, page 67.

Chapter Seven
When the veil is taken from our eyes

Not only was his [Moroni's] robe exceedingly white, but his whole person was glorious beyond description, and his countenance truly like lightning. The room was exceedingly light, but not so very bright as immediately around his person. When I first looked upon him, I was afraid; but the fear soon left me.

Joseph Smith—History 1:32

There are a number of places in the scriptures which give detailed descriptions of personages who have appeared to mortals. For example, the description of Moroni when he appeared to Joseph Smith is enlightening. The Prophet described his personage as follows (Joseph Smith—History 1:30-32):

While I was thus in the act of calling upon God, I discovered a light appearing in my room, which continued to increase until the room was lighter than at noonday, when immediately a personage appeared at my bedside, standing in the air, for his feet did not touch the floor.

He had on a loose robe of most exquisite whiteness. It was a whiteness beyond anything earthly I had ever seen; nor do I believe that any earthly thing could be made to appear so exceedingly white and brilliant. His hands were naked, and his arms also, a little above the wrist; so, also, were his feet naked, as were his legs, a little above the ankles. His head and neck were also bare. I could discover that he had no other clothing on but this robe, as it was open, so that I could see into his bosom.

> Not only was his robe exceedingly white, but his whole person was glorious beyond description, and his countenance truly like lightning. The room was exceedingly light, but not so very bright as immediately around his person. When I first looked upon him, I was afraid; but the fear soon left me.

This description is very enlightening [pun intended] to us, for it gives us an idea of the interesting features of persons from beyond the veil. Of course, Moroni was an angel, and therefore resurrected, but nonetheless we can imagine the nature of persons and the way they look on the other side of the veil. Some things to consider: the room was lighter than at noonday; the personage was standing in the air; he had a robe of exquisite whiteness; his hands, arms, feet, and legs were visible; his head and neck were bare also; his whole being was glorious beyond description; and his countenance so bright that it obviously made the entire room bright.

We also have the description of the Savior when He appeared to Joseph Smith and Oliver Cowdery in the Kirtland Temple on 3 April 1836. The revelation found in Doctrine and Covenants 110:1-3, states:

> The veil was taken from our minds, and the eyes of our understanding were opened.

> We saw the Lord standing upon the breastwork of the pulpit, before us; and under his feet was a paved work of pure gold, in color like amber.

> His eyes were as a flame of fire; the hair of his head was white like the pure snow; his countenance shone above the brightness of the sun; and his voice was as the sound of the rushing of great waters . . .

Again, we can't make too strong a comparison between the Lord Himself and people in the world of spirits, but there are features—the brightness of his countenance, for example, that may be somewhat similar.

The point I'm making here is that in the spirit world, spiritual beings will look considerably different than people in mortality. They will take upon themselves a new luster as it were; they will no doubt look brighter and more than likely shine as the noonday sun.

Brent and Wendy Top help us a great deal in understanding the nature of people in the spirit world. They have done extensive research into near-death experiences which have been reported by both Latter-day Saints and non-members alike. In their writings, they give detailed accounts of the nature and features of people on the other side of the veil. From the near death experiences they have researched, we obtain interesting insights in what people are like in the world of spirits.

In a book published in 2005[65], they describe how people seem to look, how they have such freedom of movement, how they communicate in some cases simply through thought, etc. Some of the significant points they make, briefly stated, about the nature of people in the spirit world follow:

> 1. Those beyond the veil have radiant white clothing.

> 2. It is possible that not only do people emanate light but they may very well be composed of it. They indeed appear to have a "luminescent" quality about them.

> 3. A person's righteousness seems to determine the amount of light and truth they possess.

They close one of the chapters "The Beautiful Appearance of Spirits"[66] with this powerful thought:

> And so we see that there are all levels of beauty and brilliance in the appearance and clothing of beings who inhabit the spirit world just as there are variations and gradations here on earth. However, in that realm where inward desires cannot be hidden by a mortal body, the distribution of true beauty is far more just, fair, and meaningful than on earth, where it is often a random and unearned gift. There, goodness and love are beauty itself, and

65   Top, Brent L. & Wendy C. (2005) Glimpses Beyond Death's Door: Gospel Insights into Near-death Experiences, Orem, Utah: Granite Publishing and Distribution, LLC.
66   Ibid., page 55

one is comely to the extent that he or she possesses them. Even a magnificence like Christ's may be obtained by anyone willing to pay the price.

They then quote from Moroni 7:48

> Wherefore, my beloved brethren, pray unto the Father with all the energy of heart, that ye may be filled with this love, which he hath bestowed upon all who are true followers of his Son, Jesus Christ; that ye may become the sons of God; that when he shall appear we shall be like him, for we shall see him as he is; that we may have this hope; that we may be purified even as he is pure. Amen.

I think it safe to say, that when people are righteous in mortality, they will take on, in the spirit world, a beauty and radiance far beyond what they possessed in mortality. I suppose the same is true of all people. Thus, when we think of loved ones who have passed through the veil, we might want to be envious of them and their increase of beauty and radiance.

The Tops mention other qualities[67] of people in the spirit world according to reports of those who have had near death experiences. Spirit beings seem to have unusual capacity for communication through thought transfer. In short, people in the spirit world seem to be able to communicate with one another through their thoughts. In addition, there seems to be an incredible ability to translate languages. The Tops also quote Joseph Smith and Brigham Young who suggest that the same sociability that exists in mortality will be extant in the spirit world.

As for movement and travel, people on the other side of the veil have unlimited freedom of movement; there will be no restriction. In the words of Brigham Young, "They move with ease and like lightning."

There will be an "ability to absorb, comprehend, and remember information." They will have the ability to remember masses of information and be able as well to comprehend them. With this ability, we would likely also have perfect recall.

---

67   Ibid., pages 57-78

We're grateful to the Tops for their exhaustive research and their clear and thoughtful expression.

THE FUTURE FOR EACH
OF US WILL BE GLORIOUS

Well, what to make of all this? It seems clear that people who pass to the other side of the veil will have incredible beauty and radiance; they will possess powers of communication beyond what we could ever imagine here in mortality; they will move about without restraint; have incredible intellectual powers.

And what is most comforting is that those of us who have deformities, whether small or great will not have them on that side of the veil. Some of us have little things, such as a slightly deformed foot perhaps; some may have cleft palate or some other disfiguring challenge; and others of course may have really serious deformities such as seriously deformed legs or backs. But whatever the deformity, whatever the malady, there is hope smiling brightly upon us as we contemplate the possibilities of the eternities—the next step being the world of the spirits.

One other thought is comforting. When we reach old age, we surely are plagued with wrinkles and lines of various kinds. And no matter how hard surgeons may try to call back our youthful selves, they are only partially successful. But when we go beyond the veil, we will look our optimum best, at our prime of life so to speak, and have all other qualities of perfection and beauty. It's a nice contemplation.

And then too, in old age we find ourselves bent over, often limping and staggering; we have a pain here and one there—our shoulders may be in pain, our backs may ache, and we hurt in places like our knees. Even our teeth deteriorate—many are missing as we reach into the sixties, seventies and eighties.

But not to worry, the future is glorious indeed; we can hope for perfection of body, mind and spirit as we progress to the next step in our eternal perfection.

With all of this said, however, those who remain after the death of a loved one must continue and try to adjust to the absence which death creates. We will discuss some of these adjustments and challenges in the coming chapters.

MAIN POINTS DISCUSSED IN CHAPTER SEVEN

1. People who find themselves in the spirit world will have an inner light, a luster that will make them look bright and glorious, almost beyond description.

2. It may be that they will radiate this light; indeed they may be composed of light which transcends our ability through mortal eyes to look upon it.

3. It seems also that people beyond the veil will have intellectual qualities beyond anything conceivable in mortality. In addition, they will have ability to recall information and will have a memory bank beyond what modern computers have.

4. People will be able to move about with ease, traveling to distant places and back in time to satisfy their curiosity and to fulfill assignments.

5. All of our mortal and physical infirmities will disappear once we pass through the veil.

6. The world of spirits is so attractive in every way that we should stand in awe and envy when a loved one passes away.

Chapter Eight
"Affliction is a treasure"

John Donne

Affliction is a treasure, and scarce any man hath enough of it. No man hath affliction enough that is not matured and ripened by it, and made fit for God . . . [68]

John Donne

SOME PEOPLE DIE SUDDENLY, OTHERS SUFFER FOR LONG PERIODS OF TIME

Elder Neal A. Maxwell, in his ministry, reminded us continually that our Savior loves us and is mindful of each of us[69] (see also Chapter 10). He also reminded us that it matters little that there are different "exits routes" from this mortality. He said that some people go suddenly and quickly with little warning to those left behind. On the other hand, others die only after long and painful suffering. It is interesting that we mortals seem to have little ability to figure out what these variations mean.

As for suffering, we surely cannot fully understand why it is necessary, but when we think about it, there is much to learn as we face its relentless requirements. Sometimes it takes days, and months, sometimes years of suffering before we die, but whatever the length of time required, there is something valuable to learn for the future. The Lord

---

68   Donne, John, Meditation XVII

69   Maxwell, Neal A. (1999). One More Strain of Praise, Salt Lake City, Utah: Bookcraft, page 9

has great love for us and is mindful of our suffering; and most importantly, that the Atonement is real and is such a nurturing comfort to us. It is about suffering prior to death that I now turn attention.

I recently read a story about B. West Belnap, former dean of the College of Religion at Brigham Young University. He held many important positions of leadership in both the Church and at Brigham Young University. He was a man known for his excellence in teaching, for his ability as an administrator, and for his charitable heart. The story was of particular interest to me because this wonderful man was my first religion teacher at BYU; I came to the University as a sophomore, searching for answers to many of life's questions; I was more than a little confused, struggling to find my way in the world. Brother Belnap befriended me and even showed special interest in me; I had the sense that he even cared for me. This by the way, is a gift great people seem to possess—there were probably thousands of other students who felt the same way about him.

At the time, I didn't realize that he was to suffer terribly with brain cancer prior to his death in 1967. Part of the story follows[70]:

> Doctors discovered that he had a malignant brain tumor. On May 12 and then again on July 16, 1966, he underwent surgery to remove it. He faced these trials with patience and a sense of humor . . . At the same time, however, he acknowledged that his pain was intense. He indicated that his own suffering had helped him better understand the infinite suffering and merciful atonement of our Savior . . .

> He acknowledged at this time in a letter to his mother that he was grateful for the fasting and prayers of loved ones. He then said,

> The one thought that I did want to communicate is that we place our faith completely in the Lord and then wait for Him to decide what is best for us.

> When the cancer persisted, West asked President Lee if he should keep fighting it. President Lee replied, "West, you and I .

---

70   BYU Religious Education Review (Winter 2011), pages 10-15.

. . know that life is a very precious thing . . . every minute of it, even the suffering of it . . . How do you and I know but what the suffering you're going through is a refining process by which [the] obedience necessary to exaltation is made up? . . . Live it out to the last day . . . Who knows but what the experience you are having now will pay dividends greater than all the rest of your life. Live it true to the end, and we'll bless you and pray to God that pains beyond your endurance will not be permitted by a merciful God.

There is much of great value in this story of a faithful man who had to face such terrible suffering prior to his death. In this case, Brother Belnap endured the pain and suffering with patience and dignity. We learn also that from this suffering he could more easily identify with our Savior's suffering—our suffering will never be equal to His, but we can come, because of our own, to a more full understanding of it. We learn, too, from President Lee that the suffering we have to endure is likely part of God's learning plan for us and that eventually the "the experience you are having now will pay dividends greater than all the rest of your life."

Cheryl Carson reminds us that "life is suffering." It is simply the way it is and that we have to learn to accept suffering as part of our sojourn on earth. She further says:

> Some assume that suffering is a sign that one is being punished for his weaknesses or mistakes. But if we attach tragedy or suffering to sin only, how do we explain the suffering of Christ? He who was least deserving of tribulation and torment endured the most. St. Augustine said, "God had one son on earth without sin, but never one without suffering."
>
> We needn't be confused. Trouble is the common denominator of living. Adversity is an integral part of this life—for everyone. "He destroyeth the perfect and the wicked." No matter how good or how bad you are, you will still have trouble. The rains descend on the house built on the rock as well as the house on sand (see Matthew 7:25). The scriptures also tell us, "Yet man is born into trouble, as the sparks fly upward" (Job 5:7). [71]

---

71   Carson, Cheryl (2000) The Anguish and Adventure of Adversity: Finding joy in the journey, Provo, Utah: TrueHeart Publishing, pages 1-2.

Ms. Carson tells an interesting legend of a "woman in deep sorrow over the death of her only son" who went to a holy man whom she thought could restore her son to life.

> He replied that she must first go throughout the land and gather flowers from the dooryards of those whose homes had known no sorrow. Of these flowers she was to make a garland and bring it to him.

> Time passed and finally the woman returned, but without the garland. "In all the land," she said, "I could find no homes whose families have known no sorrow. Now I can be content with my lot."

ANY SUFFERING IN MORTALITY IS PART OF OUR MORTAL PREPARATION

That being the case, we must look upon the suffering of loved ones prior to their exit into the spirit world as part of their preparation for greater blessings and opportunities which await them.

Elder Jeffrey R. Holland tells, in his characteristically brilliant way, a poignant story of the death of a beautiful thirteen-year old girl and the hope and blessing it may be for those of us left behind after the loss of a loved one. He tells of a couple, longtime friends, who laid their first-born child in the grave.

> This beautiful little thirteen-year-old girl, born just ninety days after our own first child, had fallen victim to Cockayne's syndrome a half dozen years earlier. There is no way to adequately describe the deterioration of that little body now gone. Nor is there any way to tell the patience and the pain of those parents as they carried legs that could not walk and finally fed with an eyedropper a mouth that could not swallow.

> . . . there was no . . . anguish rending the air. Standing quietly—no, peacefully—at the casket with this little family now temporarily lessened by Patti's leaving were her Beehive class, her Sunday School teacher, and a favorite teenage home teacher. There also were the two with whom her father had served in the bish-

opric. Her mother's Relief Society associates dried their tears and slipped away to prepare a family luncheon. Fellow members in the body of Christ remembered, "And whether one member suffer, all the members suffer with it" (1 Corinithians 12:26).

In that circle, these were the graveside lyrics of a loving neighbor, lines sung in this setting not for their sentiment but for their theology:

> Do you know who you are, little child of mine,
> So precious and dear to me?
> Do you know you are a part of a great design
> That is vast as eternity? . . .
> Do you know you're a child of God?
>
> Do you know where you're going, child of mine?
> Are your eyes on the road ahead?
> Do the spires of his castle gleam and shine
> Where the sun grows golden red? . . .
> You will make it, my child, I know.

Ora Pate Stewart, "To a Child"

SUFFERING TEACHES US CONCERN FOR OTHERS; REMINDS US TO BE FORGIVING

While serving a two-year mission to Armenia, my wife and I had an unusual experience which I described in a letter to our family. I cite a large part of the letter in which I explain that there is always much suffering associated with our lives in mortality. I wrote the letter in October 2003:

> Not long ago, Mother and I went to a small city in northern Armenia called Spitak. While chatting with the mayor of the city, he mentioned that there is a German military cemetery just on the outskirts of their city. He said that during the Second World War there was a large number of German prisoners of war brought here by the Russians to work in an old sugar factory and, while

here, many of them died. He added that recently, working with a German private agency (who probably paid for the project), the citizens of the city had made significant improvements to the site. They made cement rectangular graves, put large crosses on the graves which were replicas of the German Iron Cross and built a large central monument with inscriptions in Armenian and German.

We wandered around the cemetery which had been nicely developed, the graves cared for, and the monument artistically done. By my estimate, there were about 250 to 300 graves all with their crosses standing in neat rows.

As I walked around the cemetery and during a few quiet moments, I couldn't help but think of the suffering these young German men must have had to endure. They were no doubt subjected to the cruelest treatment, given little food, and forced to work for 10 or 12 hours or more each day with little rest. They probably had only basic shelter and it isn't likely that they had any kind of heating system to keep warm in the winter. Naturally, many died.

I thought, too, of the suffering these young German soldiers must have inflicted on the Russians and other people. After all, it was the Germans who took the war to Russia. They no doubt brought misery and suffering to thousands upon thousands of people in the villages and towns they captured and destroyed as they swept across Eastern Europe.

I have to say that this short experience in far off Armenia has brought to my mind that all down through human history there has been a great deal of suffering brought about by calamities of all shapes and sizes; groups of people, large and small, have had to endure plagues, pestilences, and famines; and much of these things on top of the wars and the struggles of mankind. And think too of the accompanying mental suffering.

Each of us in individual ways also seems to suffer from time to time, probably more often than we wish. My dad suffered a great deal from a terrible accident that burned his legs in molten lead. My mother suffered from osteoporosis while nearing death's door. And, in truth, I have to think that each of us, if we haven't suffered much to date, will have to cope with some kind of malady or another at some point in time. In my own case, my shoulder has really been bothering me lately which follows on a pain I've had for a long time in my neck, which follows on a pain I've had in my right hip, etc. etc. Not to mention the pain I've felt worrying about each of you and missing you and wishing I could be with you for a time. And think about some suffering I've inflicted upon you, and you upon me. And come to think of it, I guess I've caused Mother to suffer over the years because of a careless word here and a criticism there. And I must mention that she has caused me to suffer from time to time.

All of this has led me to think about our Savior and his exquisite suffering for all mankind and surely some of His suffering falls back to me. I've inflicted on him my share of sin and transgression. I guess in our fumbling way all of us have caused him suffering--all mankind has. As Jacob reminds us (2 Nephi 9:21-22), the Savior came "into the world to save all men,

> . . . for behold, he suffereth the pains of all men, yea, the pains of every living creature, both men, women, and children, who belong to the family of Adam.

> And he suffereth this that the resurrection might pass upon all men . . .

Alma also teaches the same doctrine in Alma 7: 11-13. He said, that the Savior shall go forth,

> suffering pains and afflictions and temptations of every kind; and this that the word might be fulfilled which saith he will take upon him the pains and sicknesses of his people.

. . . nevertheless the Son of God suffereth according to the flesh that he might take upon him the sins of his people, . . .

Well, knowing these things, there are a few important lessons for all of us. First, I should say that we ought to carry around in our hearts a bit of sorrow for the pain we may have caused others. We should nurture within us feelings of sorrow for whatever injury we have brought to another human being, especially those in our close circle of love. And for sure, we ought to carry feelings of sorrow for the injury we have inflicted upon our Savior.

We ought to be careful not to offend people around us, to bring any kind of suffering to them, especially the ones we love the most. We ought to try hard not to inflict on anyone something that may cause them suffering. You who are husbands surely ought to be careful how you treat your wives and not cause them to suffer in the least degree. And, you wives must be sensitive and not inflict any suffering on your husbands. In short, we need to carry in our hearts a repentant spirit for whatever degree of suffering we may have caused others.

Second, it would be a good idea to ask forgiveness of those who we may have offended. I remember a friend came to me one day and said, "Wayne, you and I have worked together for a long time. I know in the rough and tumble of life there are always things that we do that may offend others. So, I'm asking, is there anything I should apologize for?" Let's reach out to others who may suffer because of us and apologize to them.

Finally, in addition to asking other people to forgive us, we should also forgive others for what suffering they may have brought to bear on us. Actually, in this we don't have an option. The Savior said, "I, the Lord, will forgive whom I will forgive, but of you it is required to forgive all men." D&C 64:10. One thing we have noticed in Armenia which affects the Church greatly is that the people have a very difficult time forgiving one another, being decent toward one another, they are forever holding a grudge, and go out of their way to be mean spirited toward one another. I'll talk more about that at some time in the future.

For now, I love you all and pray for you continually. Love, Dad

SUFFERING MAY BE EXACTLY WHAT WE NEED FOR OUR ETERNAL PROGRESSION

We learn from these stories that suffering is our mortal lot and becomes particularly painful when a loved one approaches his or her exit time. On the other hand, as we have learned in this chapter, it may very well be that the suffering is exactly the blessing that is needed. This is hard to say, but from all that we read about suffering, there is a purpose to it and part of the learning that is required. And as President Lee notes above, the time of suffering prior to a passing of a loved one may pay great dividends for the future. By our nature, however, we as loved ones want the suffering to end; we want to expedite it, or shortcut it so as to not prolong it.

THERE ARE NO SHORTCUTS TO ETERNITY

One day in 1970, while I served as Mission President in Samoa, I read in the local newspaper that the famous Peter Snell from New Zealand was in Samoa conducting a sports camp for athletes interested in track and field. I remember being very excited that he was in Samoa since I had followed his career as the most dominate middle distance runner in the world during the decade of the Sixties. Indeed, he set many world records, was an Olympic champion and dominated the 800 meter and 1500 meter races wherever he went in the world. Anyone who had watched him run would find it difficult to erase from mind the graceful stride, the dominate power of his running. In fact, later at the end of the century, Peter Snell was voted as the sports/athlete of the century in New Zealand. I remember thinking at the time that Peter Snell could very well be voted as the world's track athlete of the Twentieth Century!

Well, to know that he was in Apia was exciting indeed. I read in the newspaper that he was staying at Aggie Grey's Hotel and would be in town for a week conducting the sports camp. I remember thinking to myself, "I wonder if I could find Mr. Snell and I wonder if he would be willing to speak to our missionaries?"

I immediately drove to the hotel and inquired whether or not Mr. Snell was around. As I chatted with the hotel clerk, lo and behold, through the front door came Peter Snell himself. I approached him, introduced myself and told a little about what I had in mind. I asked him if his schedule would allow time to speak to some of our missionaries. We would be available as an audience at his convenience.

He accepted the invitation and we arranged a time for the next day for him to speak. At the appointed time, forty of our missionaries gathered in the Pesega Ward chapel. Right on schedule, Mr. Snell arrived. I was so happy to greet him and was very pleased to introduce him to the missionaries.

He stood before us and told the following story. When he was a young man he trained to run middle distance races and soon dominated the sport for juniors in New Zealand. In due time, he was junior champion in the 1500 meter race, a feat quite remarkable given the fact that there were a host of impressive runners in New Zealand. In fact, New Zealand had produced a number of world class runners including Murray Halberg an Olympic champion and one of the greatest runners of his time.

Well, after a particular race which Peter had won, he was approached by Murray Halberg who at the time was the New Zealand Olympic coach. Mr. Halberg said that he was very impressed with his running ability, his power, his smooth stride, and in fact, he said, that Peter had without question all of the attributes of a potential world champion middle distance runner. "There is only one thing I'm not sure of," said Mr. Halberg. "I'm not sure that you have the heart, the courage to train, the persistence to be a world champion."

Peter Snell then asked, "What do I have to do to prove that I have the heart?"

Murray Halberg said, "You have to have the heart to train for long hours, the heart to discipline yourself to a careful regimen, and the ability to keep your focus on becoming a champion. You will have to overcome the loneliness that comes in long hours of training, you will have to discipline yourself to the pain that sets in while training—these are matters of the heart."

Peter asked another question. "What specifically must I do in the training regimen?"

Halberg replied, "You must train at the level other world champions train. You will have to run at least 100 miles a week as the central feature of your training. That's about 15 miles per day. That, my Friend, is a very difficult training schedule and a test of your heart!"

Peter thought for a moment and said, "I can do that. I'll do it!"

Without delay Peter began training. He laid out a running course that took him out of the city about seven and a half miles, he would then cross over to another road that he would follow that would take him back into town. It was a perfect 15 mile route.

He trained on this course day after day, month after month. Indeed it was difficult, lonely and tedious, just as Murray Halberg had warned. His "heart" was being tested. His resolve was put to the test. But he persisted. He put in the long hours of training that would eventually take him to the top of the runner's world.

He then added, "Each day when I would run out of the city, there were many cross streets that cut over to the route that would return me to the city. And you know, there were many, many days when I was tempted, especially when the pain of running would set in, to cut across, to take a short-cut."

As soon as Peter said this, one of our elders raised his hand, stood, and asked, "Mr. Snell, with respect, did you ever take that shortcut?"

There was dead silence. Peter Snell slowly looked around the room making eye contact with many of the elders. Then with a very thoughtful countenance, he began to nod his head ever so slowly. Then there appeared a slight smile on his face, and while focusing his attention fully on the elder who asked the question, he said, "Son, you can never become a world champion by taking a shortcut. No sir, you can't be a champion of anything by taking a shortcut."

This story has been such an impressive guide for me in life and it surely applies here to our discussion pertaining to the suffering we often face, or a loved one faces, prior to passing away. We want to leave this frail existence armed with whatever knowledge Heavenly Father wants to teach us, however hard that may be. And it may very well be that the suffering, not always, but often can sharpen our minds to provide for greatest learning.

MAIN POINTS DISCUSSED IN CHAPTER EIGHT

1. We don't always know why a loved one is called on to suffer prior to passing away, but we must come to realize that there is a purpose to the suffering and much to learn from it. When seen in this light, affliction is truly a treasure.

2. One purpose may be to prepare us for a great "dividend" (to use President Lee's idea), that is to say a great blessing in the future. The suffering, in other words, may be important to preparing us for the future.

3. One of the great benefits of suffering is to give us an appreciation for the Savior's suffering.

4. The suffering of a loved one prior to passing away surely gives all of us the opportunity to provide selfless service, acts of kindness, as part of the family of Latter-day Saints.

5. It may be, as a result of suffering, that we can be more charitable toward others and reach out to help them even though we may be suffering ourselves.

6. We must accept the Lord's wisdom as to the length of the suffering we or a loved one may be called on to suffer. There are no shortcuts, in other words, when we are dealing with the Lord's plan for us or a loved one.

Chapter Nine
Preparing for the inevitability of death

"The noblest aim in life is to strive to live to make other lives better and happier. Browning sounds the keynote in Paracelsus, when he says: "There is an answer to the passionate longings of the heart for fulness, and I knew it. And the answer is this: Live in all things outside yourself by love and you will have joy. That is the life of God; it ought to be our life. In him it is accomplished and perfect; but in all created things, it is a lesson learned slowly against difficulty."[72]

President David O. McKay

THE SAVIOR PREPARED FOR HIS DEATH

It is interesting that the Savior, from the very foundation of the world, prepared Himself for His eventual death. This was part of the plan from the very beginning, and as we have learned from previous chapters in this book that we, too, will all leave this mortal existence. It makes sense, then, that we likewise prepare, as did the Savior, for the inevitability of death.

This is easier said than done! None of us wants to focus too intensely on our demise, and so we mostly put off any kind of planning that would make our passing somewhat easy for those we leave behind. Of course, when a person passes away because of sudden illness or accident, we can't be prepared specifically for that time, but we can in a general way prepare ourselves for the time when, we too, pass away.

---

72 Gospel Ideals: Selections from the Discourses of David O. McKay. (1953). Salt Lake City, Utah: Deseret Book Company. Compiled by the Editors of The Improvement Era, page 134

IT MAKES SENSE THAT WE PREPARE FOR OUR EVENTUAL DEATH

In this chapter, we will suggest ideas which may help in preparing for the inevitability of death and perhaps what we can do, ahead of time, to make the occasion of our passing relaxed and somewhat happy.

Not long after my wife passed away, one of my daughters came to me and said, "Dad, death is inevitable—you are going to die at some point in time. Why not begin now to prepare your funeral program so that for all of us who are left behind, we'll have a much calmer time when you pass away." She partly said these words in jest, but was serious enough that she handed me a package of planning papers she had obtained from a mortuary so that I could begin to consider the details of my death—funeral plans, financial plans, etc. She wanted me to have things prepared when I die so that all events surrounding the funeral and my passing will be calm and joyous. Indeed, all of my children and yours will be able to celebrate the wonders of the Plan of Salvation and Redemption and Happiness when there is good planning, rather than running around making decisions after we die that in many ways distract from the greater experience of death.

WE SHOULD PUT AWAY OUR "FOOLERIES."

As the years go on, we should become more and more faithful and committed to the Gospel of Jesus Christ. There should be no doubt in our minds or anyone else's that we are fully devoted to our Father in Heaven and in His Son Jesus Christ. Nothing is more important than this kind of preparation for our eventual death.

As time passes, we should put away the things that are frivolous in our lives, put away as Elder Orson Pratt once said, the "fooleries" of life. He said, in 1873, words that should have extra meaning and application for us in our time:

> With a work of such magnitude before them, the Latter-day Saints should be wide awake, and should not have their minds engaged in those fooleries in which many indulge at the present

time. We should put these things away, and our inquiry should be "Lord how can we prepare the way before thy coming?" "How can we prepare ourselves to perform the great work which must be performed in this greatest of dispensations of the fullness of times?" "How can we be prepared to behold the Saints who lived on the earth in former dispensations, and take them by the hand and fall upon their necks and they fall upon ours, and we embrace each other?" "How can we be prepared for this?" How can all things that are in Christ Jesus, both which are in heaven and on the earth, be assembled in one grand assembly, without we are wide awake?"[73]

THE BEST PREPARATION WE CAN MAKE IS TO DO FAMILY HISTORY AND TEMPLE WORK

One way to show our full devotion and to become fully prepared for our own passing is to become faithful temple attenders, engaged in the work to save our kindred dead who are on the other side of the veil. In the King Follett speech which Joseph Smith gave[74], he said among other things:

> What promises are made in relation to the subject of the salvation of the dead? And what kind of characters are those who can be saved, although their bodies are moldering and decaying in the grave? When his commandments teach us, it is in view of eternity; for we are looked upon by God as though we were in eternity. God dwells in eternity, and does not view things as we do.

The greatest responsibility in this world that God has laid upon us is to seek after our dead. The Apostle Paul [said],

> They without us cannot be made perfect (Hebrews 11:40) for it is necessary that the sealing power should be in our hands to seal our children and our dead for the fullness of the dispensation of

---

73   Orson Pratt, Journal of Discourses, Vol. 16, p. 326, November 22, 1873
74   Teachings of the Prophet Joseph Smith, Salt Lake City, Utah: Deseret Book Company, page 356.

times—a dispensation to meet the promises made by Jesus Christ before the foundation of the world for the salvation of man.

I know of no better way to prepare ourselves for the inevitability of our own passing than to become devoted temple workers and seekers after our kindred dead. This takes much time and some money, but nothing is more important than this "greatest responsibility." This is something we should conscientiously do as part of our preparation for the eventuality of death. This is also the best remedy I can think of to help us through the mourning days following the death of a loved one.

READING SCRIPTURES IS AN ESSENTIAL PART OF OUR PREPARATION

As we grow older, we should pay much more attention to the admonitions of prophets to read scripture. Nothing is more important than being students of the Gospel so that we understand the doctrines of the Church as taught by the prophets and apostles. We should do as the Brethren have long recommended that we read the scriptures regularly and become very well acquainted with them. This kind of devotion is essential for careful and happy preparation.

This is something we should do all the days of our lives, but it should be one of the most important things we can do to prepare for death. President Hinckley said[75]:

> If you want to have a testimony of the God of heaven, read the scriptures. The Lord said, "Search the scriptures; for in them ye think ye have eternal life; and they are they which testify of me" (John 5:39). Now, if you have any questions about that, you read the scriptures, you pray, and you come to know without any question that the God of heaven lives.

> If you have any doubt about the reality of the Lord Jesus Christ, you study the gospel. You read the New Testament. You read the Book of Mormon, which testifies of the Savior. It is the

---

75   Discourses of President Gordon B. Hinckley, Volume 2, 2000-2004, Salt Lake City, Utah: The Church of Jesus Christ of Latter-day Saints, pages 495-496.

testament of the New World, borne hand in hand with the testament of the Old World. And there will come into your heart, as sure as daylight comes in the morning, a knowledge that Jesus Christ is the Son of God.

President Ezra Taft Benson counsels us in this way[76]:

> We must diligently study the scriptures. The Book of Mormon, Brigham Young said, was written on the tables of his heart and no doubt helped save him from being deceived . . .
>
> The Doctrine and Covenants is important because it contains the revelations which helped lay the foundation of this great latter-day work . . .
>
> Do we, as Saints of the Most High God, treasure the word He has preserved for us at so great a cost? . . .I bear my solemn witness that the Book of Mormon and Doctrine and Covenants contain the mind and the will of the Lord for us in these days of trial and tribulation. They stand with the Bible to give witness of the Lord and His work. These books contain the voice of the Lord to us in these latter days. May we turn to them with full purpose of heart and use them in the way the Lord wishes them to be used.

REGULAR AND SUSTAINED PRAYER WILL HELP US PREPARE FOR OUR EVENTUAL DEATH

Being faithful in the Church, attending to our meetings and duties, being regular temple attenders; and spending regular time in the scriptures will help us prepare all through our lives for the inevitability of death. It's likely that when all these things are done, prayer will be an important component in our lives. I won't elaborate too much here, but without prayer, we will find ourselves drifting away from our focus on preparation for life eternal. Prayers will be heard; they will be answered; and Heavenly Father will be with us all the days of our lives.

---

76   Benson, Ezra Taft (1988), The Teachings of Ezra Taft Benson, Salt Lake City, Utah: Bookcraft, page 42.

President Hinckley taught us about the importance of prayer in a wonderful address on the April 6, 2003 in the Sunday Afternoon Session of General Conference. He said in part:

> . . . I offer a plea that each of us will seek to live closer to the Lord and to commune with Him more frequently and with increased faith.

> Fathers and mothers, pray over your children. Pray that they may be shielded from the evils of the world. Pray that they may grow in faith and knowledge. Pray that they may be directed toward lives that will be profitable and good. Husbands, pray for your wives. Express unto the Lord your gratitude for them, and plead with Him in their behalf. Wives, pray for your husbands. Many of them walk a very difficult road with countless problems and great perplexities. Plead with the Almighty that they may be guided, blessed, protected, and inspired in their righteous endeavors.

> Pray for peace in the earth, that the Almighty, who governs the universe, will stretch forth His hand and let His Spirit brood upon the people, that the nations may not rage one against another.

> Pray for the weather . . .

> Pray for wisdom and understanding as you walk the difficult paths of your lives . . .

> Let us be a prayerful people. Let us bring up our children "in the nurture and admonition of the Lord" (Enos 1:1).

People who regularly pray receive comfort to the soul. All of our lives should be marked by prayer and supplication to the Lord for his tender mercies. It is through prayer that we take our concerns and our hopes before God the Eternal Father, who responds in His own way, to our eternal blessing.

Prayer is the Soul's Sincere Desire

Prayer is the soul's sincere desire,
Uttered or unexpressed,
The motion of a hidden fire,
That trembles in the breast.

Prayer is the burden of a sigh,
The falling of a tear,
The upward glancing of an eye,
When none but God is near.

Prayer is the simplest form of speech,
That infant lips can try,
Prayer, the sublimest strains that reach,
The majesty on high.

Prayer is the Christian's vital breath,
The Christian's native air,
His watchword at the gates of death,
He enters heav'n with prayer.

All of the things mentioned above are part of what faithful Latter-day Saints do regularly; and because they are faithful, their lives are prepared for a blessed departure from this life.

SERVICE IS CRUCIAL AS WE PREPARE TO LEAVE MORTALITY

I want to make one other point in terms of overall preparation for the day of our departure or the departure of a loved one from this life. I have learned over many years that the best way to bless our lives, not that we do things necessarily for blessings, is to serve others. All around us are people who need help of one kind or another. This is another important way to prepare ourselves for the work that goes on in the world of spirits.

President Monson has been teaching us over many decades that Latter-day Saints define their lives by rendering Christ-like service to those in need. We learn from him that service, saintly service, is an important quality of our membership in the Church. It is through service that our final judgment may depend; indeed it may determine our eternal reward.

As you have read repeatedly in this book, if we are true and faithful in living our lives according to the commandments, all will be well with us; and we will be prepared when the time comes to go down into our own graves rejoicing.

MAIN POINTS DISCUSSED IN CHAPTER NINE

1. As the years go on, we should become more and more faithful and committed to the Gospel of Jesus Christ.

2. One of the most important things we can do to prepare for our own passing is to become serious about doing genealogy and temple work. After all, the Prophet Joseph Smith made it clear that our most important responsibility in this life is to seek after our kindred dead.

3. Regular scripture reading should be an important part of our preparation. Hopefully, this has been a lifetime commitment with all of its myriad blessings.

4. Sincere and daily prayer should be a part also of our lives and will do much to help us prepare for our own passing.

5. And service is also a way to prepare for the eternities since helping others is part and parcel of what we'll be doing for the welfare of the children of men.

Chapter Ten
All are known unto God

And it came to pass that the people of God were joined that day by more than the number who had been slain; and those who had been slain were righteous people, therefore we have no reason to doubt but what they were saved.

Alma 24:26

THE SAVIOR KNOWS
EACH OF HIS CHILDREN

Elder Neal A Maxwell noted in Chapter Eight that our Savior loves us and is mindful of each one of us.[77] He seems to suggest that the Savior is aware of each person on the earth, and the timing and the manner of departure are all part of His Redeeming love and grace. This is, of course, hard for us mortals because we want to be in charge of the timing and the manner of departure from mortality. Fortunately, we don't have the power to make these decisions; they are best left to our Savior's wisdom and mercy.

If Brother Maxwell is right, and I believe that he is with all my heart, then what about when a massacre occurs; when thousands are killed quickly and suddenly, perhaps over a span of a few days? Is our Savior aware of each person? Yes, He is! Is He also aware of perpetrators of these awful and painful crimes? Yes, He is!

Most people are aware of what is called the Rape of Nanking, one of the most horrible massacres in the history of the world. From late December 1937 to early spring of 1938 perhaps as many as 300,000

---

77   Maxwell, Neal A. (1999). One More Strain of Praise, Salt Lake City, Utah: Bookcraft, page 9.

people were slaughtered by soldiers of the Japanese Imperial Army. Most of the people were civilians. Not only were they put to death, but there were numerous acts of barbarity—rape, looting, arson and the execution of prisoners of war and of course, civilians.

What is not so well known is the Babi Yar Massacre which occurred near Kiev, Ukraine on 29-30 September, 1941 by a special team of German SS troops who were supported by other German units as well as collaborators and Ukrainian police. There were 33,771 Jewish civilians shot at what is termed the "largest single massacre in the history of the Holocaust." And if that weren't enough, there were another 100,000 people massacred in the months that followed in this area of the Ukraine.[78]

Over the long stretches of history, there have been many awful incidents of murder and massacre. One thinks, for example, of the hordes who came out of Mongolia, under the leadership of Genghis Khan, who killed and pillaged their way across eastern Europe. In most cases, they took the spoils of their capture, and put to death those people who had resisted them, perhaps millions.

And who can forget the awful atrocities of the First and Second World Wars when countless millions of people were put to death. And there have been other atrocities as well--the Holocaust; the genocide of 1.5 million Armenians in Turkey; the Pol Pot atrocities where he massacred one third of the population of the small country of Cambodia?

The questions which come to mind when thinking of these awful atrocities are sobering indeed. And is the Savior aware of all these people who crossed over from mortality to the spirit world in a relatively short period of time?

The exits routes of many millions of people have been through murder and massacre. We are comforted by the fact that our loving Father in Heaven is intensely aware of all of His children; that he would bless these people who met tragedy with the same love as anyone else who has crossed over to the world of spirits. And what's more, He loves those who were the cause of the massacres. Indeed, none are beyond His love and mercy!

---

78   http://www.bukisa.com/articles/29175 12 infamous massacres in history#ixzzlSCbI2I nw

THE SAINTS IN BOOK OF MORMON TIMES AND LATTER-DAY SAINTS ARE NO STRANGERS TO ATROCITY

In the case of Saints of God, we've surely known our times of massacre and murder. The Book of Mormon is replete with stories of the catastrophe of war and turbulence. For example, one of the most heart rending stories in the Book of Mormon has to do with the Lamanite members who refused to take up their arms once they had become converted to the Gospel. On one occasion, their Lamanite enemies came upon them and slaughtered more than 1000 of them.

Here's the way the story appears in the Book of Mormon. Please see Alma 24:21-22.

> Now when the people saw that they were coming against them they went out to meet them, and prostrated themselves before them to the earth, and began to call on the name of the Lord; and thus they were in this attitude when the Lamanites began to fall upon them, and began to slay them with the sword.

> And thus without meeting any resistance, they did slay a thousand and five of them; and we know that they are blessed, for they have gone to dwell with their God.

You know the rest of the story; how the Lamanites became pricked in their hearts, threw down their weapons of war and many of them were converted to the Gospel. Alma continues:

> And it came to pass that the people of God were joined that day by more than the number who had been slain; and those who had been slain were righteous people, therefore we have no reason to doubt but what they were saved (v. 26).

I mention one more Book of Mormon story here. According to Mormon, thousands and tens of thousands were slain in the great battle of Cumorah. We can hardly imagine such slaughter (See Mormon 6:10-15):

> And it came to pass that my men were hewn down, yea, even my ten thousand who were with me, and I fell wounded in the

midst; and they passed by me that they did not put an end to my life.

And when they had gone through and hewn down all my people save it were twenty and four of us, (among whom was my son Moroni) and we having survived the dead of our people, did behold on the morrow, when the Lamanites had returned unto their camps, from the top of the hill Cumorah, the ten thousand of my people who were hewn down, being led in the front by me.

And we also behold the ten thousand of my people who were led by my son Moroni.

And behold, the ten thousand of Gidgiddonah had fallen, and he also in the midst.

And Lamah had fallen with his ten thousand; and Gilgal had fallen with his ten thousand; and Limhah had fallen with his ten thousand; and Jeneum had fallen with his ten thousand; and Cumenihah, and Moronihah, and Antionum, and Shjiblom, and Shem, and Josh, had fallen with their ten thousand each.

And it came to pass that there were ten more who did fall by the sword, with their ten thousand each . . .

The death toll here is shocking. And when you add up the women and children who also perished, the numbers are staggering; all having died in a relatively short period of time—perhaps a few days.

Our Savior knows and loves each one of God's children and is pleased to welcome them to the world of spirits where they can begin to progress in a more peaceful sphere. They would have all passed through the veil in a very orderly and peaceful way; they would have been welcomed and were assured that they were taking their next step in their progression. So, we come to a very interesting conclusion here: Heavenly Father is aware of His children, whether one passes through the veil or millions, they all enter the world of spirits in an orderly way, even though they may have died in a disorderly way; He accommodates all in love who pass through the veil.

WE MORTALS HAVE A DIFFICULT TIME SEEING THE BIG PICTURE

Our problem, as is also implied in Elder Maxwell's thoughts as noted above, is that the vast majority of people can't see the end from the beginning; we cannot see the big picture. We sometimes look upon death not in an eternal way but rather in an immediate way—we look upon it as related to me, or I, or us! When this happens, we can easily become angry at the Lord's timing or we can become depressed when we lose a loved one because "his or her loss" affects those who stay on in mortality.

Why is it that some people go to the other side of the veil suddenly; and why is it that some go slowly? Or, why are there atrocities or other acts of violence that take millions of lives? I guess the safe answer is that we don't know; we have to trust in the Lord's mercy and grace.

We have to be careful here. We often hear people say, "Well, my sweetheart is needed on the other side." Or, when a young returned missionary passes away, we can't assume that he is doing a "special" work on the other side of the veil. There is, of course, no evidence of this. About the most important answer to this situation is that our faithful loved ones are going to be busy—they will be preaching the Gospel to untold millions who have departed this life without an understanding of the truth, or without having heard the true Gospel. And their passing is dictated and under the direction of the Savior Himself.

The point we must strongly make here is that the Savior is in charge. He knows all of his children and counts each unto himself; he loves them and has concern for them. It doesn't matter either how they go through the veil, what is important is that he knows them all. Impossible you say? No, He knows us all; He is in charge; each one is counted unto Him.

MAIN POINTS DISCUSSED
IN CHAPTER TEN

1. Some people are required to pass through the veil suddenly, even quickly, while some are required to pass over to the other side after a great deal of suffering.

2. Why there are variations in the "exit routes," we can't be sure; we must trust in the Lord's wisdom and love for each of us.

3. Even though there are great atrocities where millions are slaughtered, they are known unto our Savior, each one.

4. It seems to be the lot of God's children in mortality to suffer all kinds of affliction, even massacres and brutality. Why this is so, we cannot be sure.

5. No matter the number who are called to leave mortality in mass or individually, in any given time, we can be sure that God knows and loves each.

Chapter Eleven
Preparing for a happy reunion on the other side of the veil

As From the Darkening Gloom[79]

As from the darkening gloom a silver dove
Upsoars, and darts into the Eastern light,
On pinions that nought moves but pure delight,
So fled thy soul into the realms above,
Regions of peace and everlasting love;
Where happy spirits, crown'd with circlets bright
Of starry beam, and gloriously bedight,
Taste the high joy none but the blest can prove.
There thou or joinest the immortal quire
In melodies that even Heaven fair
Fill with superior bliss, or, at desire
Of the omnipotent Father, cleavest the air
On holy message sent—What pleasures higher?
Wherefore does any grief our joy impair?

John Keats

THOUGHTS OF HAPPY REUNIONS ON THE OTHER SIDE OF THE VEIL SHOULD MOTIVATE US TO BE FAITHFUL ON THIS SIDE

For faithful Latter-day Saints, the contemplation of a happy re-union with family and friends once we pass to the other side of the veil is sweet and glorious. We can quite easily envision meeting loved-

---

79   The Complete Poetry and Selected Prose of John Keats (1951). New York: The Modern Library, page 18.

ones who have passed before us and contemplate the hugs and kisses awaiting us in a spirit of love and happiness. In the wonderful realm of the Spirit World, the faithful and humble followers of the Lord Jesus Christ will be greeted with singing and dancing by our kindred dead, those who were faithful themselves. And what a reunion it will be with those for whom we have done temple work. The contemplation of these happy reunions should motivate us to live worthily on this side of the veil.

As I've pondered the nature of the reunions that must take place on the other side of the veil, I have envisioned the joy and happiness that will be in the hearts of all the people in such a gathering. Each reunion, I suppose, will be filled with love and gratitude.

Quite often in mortality, we get a glimpse of happy reunions when friends and loved ones meet. Oftentimes, families hold reunions on a regular basis in an effort to help all members of an extended family remain in touch with one another. In most cases, these reunions are happy and bring a lot of good fellowship to family members. As happy as these reunions are, for me, the most touching and poignant reunions usually take place at airports when a successful young missionary returns to his or her family—there is simply nothing quite like it—the joy is inexpressible. When one of our daughters or sons returned from missions and walked into the airport terminal; in no other place is the emotion so overwhelming and poignant.

So, we might be able to gauge the happiness of those future reunions in the Spirit World by comparing them with happy reunions we have on this side of the veil. Even so, however wonderful mortal reunions are, they will likely pale when compared to the scene which will open to us beyond the veil. With that said, the following is a touching story of the kind of reunions that often occur at airports around the world when missionaries return from their fields of labor. This story[80], told over and over again, may give us an inkling of what to expect when a loved one passes through the veil.

> Glancing at one of the nearby gates, I recognized a familiar
> sight. I could tell from the group of missionary friends and family

---

80   Author Unknown

gathered near the window that an elder was coming home today. There was a feeling of excitement mixed with nervousness, and as I turned to go that feeling caught hold of me. I thought, this is one of life's special moments, why not take a moment or two to watch and enjoy.

And so I turned back to the window, I set my briefcase down, and tried to pick out that returning young man's closest friends and members of his immediate family.

There was his father, obviously a man of the soil and well acquainted with hard work. He looked as out of place as he felt in a worn, slightly tattered sport jacket that was Sunday best and probably never out of the closet otherwise.

His mother hovered nearby, slight of face and figure, her hazel eyes continually scanning the horizon for that long awaited plane. And I spied several younger brothers who had apparently forgotten, for the moment, what today was and were amusing themselves by running and playing and exploring as children are apt to do when left momentarily unwatched in a place with as many interesting sights and people as the airport.

And of course, there was the girlfriend. She had not forgotten what was happening today. She had waited two years and wasn't about to miss this.

From the way each of them took a step closer to the glass, I knew that the plane they were waiting for had landed and was now taxing slowly, ever so slowly toward the terminal. I began to wonder which one of these would be the first to make a break for the long awaited reunion with the returning young man.

My first guess was his mother who from the way she was wringing what had once been a silk hanky obviously needed something to hold on to. Then again, maybe one of those little brothers would look up from their play just long enough to see who was getting off the plane and would run with childlike exuberance to get a hug from big brother's familiar arms.

I think the girlfriend wanted to most of all, but then, well, two years is a long time and one doesn't want to appear too anxious. Still her breathing was erratic and I wondered if I should call for a paramedic and some oxygen.

I could tell from the light that entered their eyes that the awaited young Elder had just appeared on the ramp. He was tall and straight and obviously knew the sacrifice this mission had been for his folks. It had made him the missionary he was supposed to be. He made his way strong, yet humble down the steps and towards the door and then it happened.

Someone broke, someone ran, someone couldn't stand the sight of him any longer without being with him. It wasn't his mother or his girlfriend and his two little brothers were still too busy with their legos and cherrios to even notice.

That big bear of a father threw an elbow into the ribs of the security guard and ran, just ran onto the flight apron to meet his son. The son's eyes clouded with tears and he barely had time to drop his bags before that blur of his father was upon him.

Now the oxygen earlier contemplated for the girlfriend could have been put to better use by the retuning young man, as his father's embrace lifted him, big as he was, clear off the ground.

And for a second, all eternity listened and the Salt Lake City airport became the center of the universe.

You know, at a time like this, it was not too hard for me to imagine that returning son saying, "Father, I've done the work you sent me forth to do, receive now my spirit unto thee." And that proud father proclaiming, "This is my beloved son, in whom I am well pleased, in whom I have glorified my name."

Now I don't know what kind of boots our Heavenly Father wears as he works the fields of eternity, but I know that the scenes of that airport occurred once long after a well-served mission and even God, the Eternal Father, sent out his own Son to serve, and to suffer, and to sacrifice.

KEEPING THE COMMANDMENTS ASSURES US OF A GLORIOUS REUNION

When we read of happy reunions on this side of the veil, such as the one I have told above, it may not be too difficult to imagine the happy reunion which awaits us on the other side of the veil. And so we can ask, "Who will be there to greet us?" "Will just a few of our immediately family be gathered?" These and other similar questions come to mind as we allow ourselves to ponder our future reunion in the Spirit World. I answer these questions in this way: We have to remember that there are many, many more of our family members on the other side of the veil than on this side. The gathering of them could be huge, and many of the people will be perfect strangers to us, but they will be our loved ones nonetheless; they will be family.

No doubt the reunions will be very happy occasions if we have been true to the covenants we have made on this side of the veil and if we have made the effort to understand and have faith in the atoning sacrifice of our Savior Jesus Christ. We have to accept the fact, I think, that our faithfulness in keeping the commandments of God in mortality will qualify us for the happiest of reunions when we enter the world of the spirits. The reunions will be especially happy if we made the effort to understand the reality of the Atonement of our Savior Jesus Christ—and all other doctrines which have been mentioned in this book.

I believe the nature of the reunions on the other side of the veil has something to do with our behavior on this side. There is much we don't understand about this, but I think it safe to say that keeping the commandments strictly in this life will assure the happiest of reunions on the other side. It should go without saying that we ought to be strict in keeping the commandments, knowing full well that by doing so will be to our everlasting advantage, the very moment we step into the eternities. From Doctrine and Covenants 130:18-21 these thoughts are confirmed:

> Whatever principle of intelligence we attain unto in this life, it will rise with us in the resurrection.
>
> And if a person gains more knowledge and intelligence in this life through his diligence and obedience than another, he will have so much the advantage in the world to come.
>
> There is a law, irrevocably decreed in heaven before the foundations of this world, upon which all blessings are predicated—
>
> And when we obtain any blessing from God, it is by obedience to that law upon which it is predicated.

Brother Maxwell makes a point we made earlier in this chapter, that we ought to do all in our power to encourage our family members and friends to be true and faithful in the keeping of the God's commandments. He continues:

> Therefore, in view of how vital mercy is, a person should take exceeding care that his mortal activities do not take him in an opposite developmental direction. Desensitizing circumstances, for example, will not help us in fostering the attribute of mercy. Neither will striving for status and preeminence, nor cutthroat competition, nor macho brusqueness! Such situations and expressions are to be shunned, for these will make us strangers to the Master and His mercy (Mosiah 5:13).

It's a little hard to imagine the wonder and the joy of those happy reunions. However, the more we labor for our kindred dead in the temple, we can more clearly imagine what it will be like, more so if we are not acquainted with them through the work we do in the temple. This labor of love keeps us interested in them and focuses our attention on them—"Who will be there to meet us? What are they like? Have they accepted the work we have done for them? Will they be glad to see us? How will they greet us when we see them?"

We've all been to funerals of faithful members. There is mourning of course, but for the most part, the funerals are happy occasions—we send the dead on their way with happy hearts and into the arms of loved ones and friends on the other side of the veil.

Brigham Young said,

> We have more friends behind the veil than on this side, and they will hail us more joyfully than you were ever welcomed by your parents and friends in this world; and you will rejoice more when you meet them than you ever rejoiced to see a friend in this life.

And the Prophet Joseph Smith said,

> I have a father, brothers, children, and friends who have gone to a world of spirits. They are only absent for a moment. They are in the spirit, and we shall soon meet again . . . When we depart, we shall hail our mothers, fathers, friends, and all whom we love, who have fallen asleep in Jesus . . . It will be an eternity of felicity.[81]

Brent and Wendy Top bring very helpful information to our discussion. In their book, quoted extensively in Chapter Seven, they say, in a chapter entitled, "Welcome Home:"

> Since the restoration of the Gospel, Latter-day Saints have held out to the world the hope of "going home" to live with their Father in Heaven again after the resurrection, as they did before they were born into mortality. Along with this, they have been taught that both there and in the pre-resurrection spirit world the faithful Saints will be reunited with their friends and family members who have preceded them. Prophets, both ancient and modern, have taught that, if we have been righteous, our relationships there will be even more gratifying than they are here.[82]

We presume, in addition to the happy reunions on the other side, there will be many sober reunions as well. Although all reunions will be full of love and compassion, some won't be all that glorious, especially

81   Quoted from Top, Brent L. and Wendy, C (2005). Glimpses Beyond Death's Door: Gospel insights into near-death experiences. Orem, Utah: Granite Publishing and Distribution, LLC., pages 209-210

82   Ibid., page 209

for someone who has passed away and has been rebellious and has been disobedient to God's commandments. We send them off to the other side with our best wishes, and hope for a merciful God to give them every opportunity to progress. In this case, I suppose we should rejoice. We can imagine loving family members there to greet them; loving people who will take them under their wings and guide them along on a path of progression. We hope for them, yearn for them and know they are loved and cherished as they enjoy the fellowship of loved ones.

Again, Elder Neal A. Maxwell helps us understand God's infinite mercy and compassion toward His children. He suggests that our circle of love may be much larger than we anticipate. In addition to welcoming family and loved ones, we may find out once on the other side of the veil that there are a host of people (in our family and otherwise) who will be assembled there. Brother Maxwell says[83]:

> In God's infinite mercy and generosity, "the glory of the teles-
> tial" will surpass "all understanding" (D&C 76:89). Furthermore,
> our family circles, when finally assembled in the celestial world
> to come, may yet be larger than some currently distressed and
> disappointed parents may now imagine; late arrivals, after having
> paid a severe price, may constitute more than just a few. "Oh, the
> greatness of the mercy of our God" (2 Nephi 9:19).

THE HAPPIEST OF ALL REUNIONS TOOK PLACE WHEN THE SAVIOR OF THE WORLD PASSED INTO THE SPIRIT WORLD

Without question, the happiest of all reunions occurred when our Savior passed through the veil into the arms of His Father. Not only was the joy beyond imagination for the Father and the Son, but for all mankind, especially those beyond the veil. President Hinckley describes, briefly, the happy reunion which followed the death and burial of the Savior in the tomb. We remember that Mary Magdalene and the

---

83   Maxwell, Neal A. (1999). <u>One More Strain of Praise</u>, Salt Lake City, Utah: Bookcraft, Inc., pages 60-61).

other Mary discovered an empty tomb; an angel appeared to them and announced that the Son of God was not there:

> "He is not here, but is risen: remember how he spake unto you when he was yet in Galilee,
>
> Saying, The Son of man must be delivered into the hands of sinful men, and be crucified, and the third day rise again" (Luke 24:5-7).
>
> These simple words—"He is not here, but is risen"—have become the most profound in all literature. They are the declaration of the empty tomb. They are the fulfillment of all He had spoken concerning rising again. They are the triumphant response to the query facing every man, woman, and child who was ever born to earth.

President Hinckley then puts before us an image of the happy reunion between the Father and the Son. He says:

> The risen Lord spoke to Mary, and she replied. He was not an apparition. This was not imagination. He was real, as real as He had been in mortal life. He did not permit her to touch Him. He had not yet ascended to His Father in Heaven. That would happen shortly. What a reunion it must have been, to be embraced by the Father, who loved Him and who also must have wept for Him during His hours of agony.

TEMPLE WORK MAY BE THE KEY TO THE HAPPY REUNIONS

If we attend the temple regularly, it is interesting to see people, mostly old but a few who are younger, who are intense in their work in behalf of the dead. I have seen older patrons who go to the temple day after day working for the salvation of their kindred dead; and not just for their own kindred dead but for others as well. They obviously know, these faithful temple workers, that those on the other side of the veil are rejoicing when their work is accomplished in the holy temple.

Doesn't it also make sense that when one of these faithful temple workers passes on, the rejoicing that will take place on the other side of the veil will be beyond description? Do we not think that when the dead are given a sort of "second chance" because of the faithful work in the temple, their happiness will know no bounds? Their appreciation and love for the person who did their temple work can only be imagined. Hence, when a person goes beyond the veil, one who has done such a noble work in the temple, the reunion will be joyous.

The reunion with family members will likely be the most joyous. For it is likely that much of the temple work a faithful saint has done will be for his or her own kindred dead. Imagine someone who has searched for years for a missing link in a family genealogy, who has found that link, and when he passes on can we imagine the reunion, the happiness on the part of both the giver and the receiver? Is it possible to comprehend the gratitude of a family member on the other side of the veil who has waited for perhaps centuries and then suddenly meets the one who has done his or her temple work? Can we imagine their gratitude?

HAPPY WILL BE THE REUNION, BUT IT WON'T BE AN ALL-NIGHT PARTY

There is a mistaken notion which floats around the Church, that the spirit world will be a time of rest which we interpret in mortality as "do nothing." I've even seen an obituary with a statement, "Gone fishing." On the other side of the veil, we won't be fishing; we'll be working—working out our own salvation, or helping work out the salvation of others. So, we won't be resting for long, based on the evidence we have been given by prophetic utterances. Our bodies will be enlivened and invigorated for the work, and there will be plenty of work to do to help our Savior preach the Gospel. In fact, there is a great irony here—the harder we work on this side of the veil in building the Kingdom of God, the harder we'll probably work on the other side—this is not your usual image of the "rest" promised when we pass away. The harder we work on this side of the veil, the harder we will likely have to work on the other side—but this is the kind of work that will be very rewarding and bring the greatest happiness.

Confirming the idea of being busy in the Spirit World, President Wilford Woodruff gives us the following:

> Joseph Smith visited me a great deal after his death, and taught me many important principles . . . I saw him at the door of the temple in heaven. He came to me and spoke to me. He said he could not stop to talk with me because he was in a hurry. The next man I met was Father Smith; he could not talk with me because he was in a hurry. I met a half a dozen brethren who had held high positions on earth, and none of them could stop to talk with me because they were in a hurry. I was much astonished. By and by I saw the Prophet again and got the privilege of asking him a question.

> "Now," said I, "I want to know why you are in a hurry. I have been in a hurry all my life; but I expected my hurry would be over when I got into the kingdom of heaven, if I ever did."

> Joseph said: "I will tell you, Brother Woodruff. Every dispensation that has had the priesthood on the earth and has gone into the celestial kingdom has had a certain amount of work to do to prepare to go to the earth with Savior when he goes to reign on the earth. We have not. We are the last dispensation, and so much work has to be done, and we need to be in a hurry in order to accomplish it.[84]

All of us who are faithful in keeping the commandments of God and making every effort to build the Kingdom of God on the earth, will hopefully have the same privilege in the world of spirits, that of working hard for the eventual return of the Savior to the world.

Robert Millet and Joseph McConkie suggest that although the world of the spirits is a place of "rest" it is a rest from the cares and sorrows of mortality not necessarily a rest in the sense of doing noth-

---

84   Deseret Weekly, 53:642-43 (October 19, 1896); cited in <u>Discourses of Wilford Woodruff</u>, ed., G. Homer Durham, (Salt Lake City: Bookcraft, Inc. 1946, 1969), pp. 288-89.

ing. It surely can't be when one considers the great responsibility that will be on the shoulders of the faithful Saints of God to preach the Gospel in the Spirit World. Their statement about "A Place of Rest" is important:

> After teaching his son Corianton concerning the journey of spirits—righteous and wicked—into the spirit world, Alma continued: "And then shall it come to pass, that the spirits of those who are righteous are received into a state of happiness, which is called paradise, a state of rest, a state of peace, where they shall rest from all their troubles and from all care, and sorrow" (Alma 40:12 italics added). We thus see that paradise is the abode of the righteous in the world of spirits, a "state of happiness," a place hereafter where the spirits of the faithful "expand in wisdom, where they have respite from all their troubles, and where care and sorrow do not annoy." Those things which burdened the obedient—the worldly cares and struggles, the vicissitudes of life—are shed with the physical body. Paradise is a place where the spirit is free to think and act with a renewed capacity and with the vigor and enthusiasm which characterized one in his prime. Though a person does not rest per se from the work associated with the plan of salvation . . . at the same time he is delivered from those cares and worries associated with a fallen world and a corrupt body.[85]

So I think that the reunions must of necessity be quite brief. After all, there is a great deal of work to do on the other side of the veil. As previously noted, there will be much missionary work that goes on in the Spirit World to prepare people to accept the Gospel. Then they will be busily engaged in temple work. This is, obviously, the main work that goes on and there appears to be full energy devoted to it. So, as I think about reunions, I imagine a happy, but brief reunion when a loved one reaches the other side. We remember Brigham Young being carried away in the spirit and had a vision of his great and dear friend Joseph Smith. Joseph was so busy that he could hardly give his friend the time of day as he had so much work to do for his kindred dead and to help prepare the world for the Second Coming of Jesus. So, it

---

85   Millet, Robert L & McConkie, Joseph Fielding (1986), The Life Beyond, Salt Lake City, Utah: Deseret Book, page 18.

appears to me, that whereas the reunions on the other side will be glorious and happy, they will be brief as there is a great deal of work to do.

MAIN POINTS DISCUSSED
IN CHAPTER ELEVEN

1. The greatest and happiest reunion in the history of the world would have taken place when Jesus returned to Heavenly Father after having accomplished His mission on earth.

2. We have many happy reunions in mortality which can only give us an inkling of the great joy and happiness which happens when a loved one passes away into the spirit world.

3. Obviously, the degree to which we are happy seems to relate to the faithfulness we have exhibited in mortality. As Brother Maxwell has said, we ought to be very careful about what we do with opportunities in this life.

4. There will be much work to do on the other side, so after a brief reunion, there will be much preaching of the Gospel and preparing people for temple work, and working to prepare for the Savior's eventual return to the earth.

Chapter Twelve
Moving beyond guilt and regret at the passing of a loved one

If you could hie to Kolob
In the twinkling of an eye
And then continue onward
With the same speed to fly,
Do you think that you could ever,
Through all eternity,
Find out the generation
Where Gods began to be?

Or see the grand beginning,
Where space did not extend?
Or view the last creation,
Where Gods and matter end?
Methinks the Spirit whispers,
"No, man has found pure space,
Nor seen the outside curtains,
Where nothing has a place.

The works of God continue,
And worlds have lives abound;
Improvement and progression
Have one eternal round
There is no end to matter,
There is no end to space,
There is no end to spirit,
There is no end to race. [86]

WE ARE SURELY NOT PERFECT CREATURES

In the rough and tumble of life, we sometimes offend people, sometimes inadvertently and of course sometimes by intent. Throughout a marriage, for example, whereas our intent is to create a perfect relationship, this is often not possible because of some profound differences we may carry with us throughout life, and so, often times, we don't have a perfect marriage. There may be disagreements, even some arguments that sometimes are not resolved with other family members. Many times we may offend by being unaware of our partner's needs and desires, sometimes we may know about their desires, but don't, for whatever reason, fulfill those desires. Such is life.

In addition, during a prolonged illness which culminates in the death of a loved one, we may offend, may not be as helpful or comforting as we could have been, again for whatever reason. And so, when a loved one passes away, there may be some guilt or regret. I know of a case, for example, where a man who had cared for his wife over a long stretch of time, but when his loved one passed away he wasn't at her side, rather he had gone to meet a need out of the home. He was crushed that he wasn't there when she actually passed away and so had some regret that he wasn't at her side at the moment when death occurred.

There are thousands of possibilities when we may have been less than perfect in our relationship with people. How many times, for example, has a parent argued with a son who slams the door on his way out of the home, only to be killed in an auto accident before amends can be made.

We must accept the fact that we are, as we all are aware, living with imperfections and weaknesses. We are not perfect beings, and that is why we have come to earth to learn to become so—this doesn't happen for any of us over night, it really takes a lifetime of effort and adjustment. Elder Robert D. Hales explains our lifelong task of improvement in this interesting way:

> As lifelong learners we see the connection between what we
> have learned in the past, what we are learning now, and what we

can learn in the future. We draw on all we have learned in the past to help us continue learning and growing. Yet we do not dwell in the past. We are always open to new concepts that are endorsed by the Spirit of Truth. We seek this new knowledge and welcome it, even when it requires us to change and grow.

That change might be expressed in this way: We spend our lives doing better than our best! Our best today is not our best tomorrow. Our best today is never our best tomorrow, for what we learn and do today changes our capacity. Our progress depends upon doing better today, even though yesterday's "better" seemed all that was possible at the time.[87]

THERE IS ALWAYS LOTS OF ROOM FOR IMPROVEMENT

Improvement must be our focused effort in this life, so if there is some regret or guilt at the passing of a loved one, we have to mostly chalk up these things to our mortal nature. In other words, there is not much we can do about the regret that we may experience at the passing of a loved one, except to try to be better people, not falling into the traps that created the regrets in the first place. For example, let us suppose that during the illness that may have claimed our loved one, we failed to make the person as comfortable on a given day as we could have—we may have been overly tired ourselves, or whatever. So when the loved one passes away, we may have some regret, even some guilt that we could have done better. From these small and seemingly insignificant things to perhaps major arguments or major differences just before the passing of a loved one, we may carry with us disappointment with ourselves—we could all do better!

There are a myriad of possibilities where we could have done better, some of which do lead to regret and guilt, but we have to realize that we are living in an imperfect world, being imperfect ourselves, and we don't always do things that with hindsight, we could have done better. Such is the nature of our existence in this imperfect world.

---

87   Hales, Robert D. (2010). Return: Four phases of our mortal journey home, Salt Lake City, Utah: Deseret Book, page 370.

Elder Robert D. Hales continues to be helpful here:

> Besides sorrowing for the passing of loved ones, sometimes we experience the sorrow of guilt for what we might have done to prevent death or better support and comfort the dying in the twilight of their lives. Some may even wonder whether they might have saved their family member or friend if they had only been more diligent or exercised more faith in their behalf.
>
> We should not blame ourselves or let guilt compound our grief when a loved one passes away. I once heard President Spencer W. Kimball teach that while we can shorten our lives by our actions, we cannot lengthen our lives one second more than the time that is granted to us to be on earth. There is a time appointed for each of us to leave this world (see D&C 42:48), which means that as long as no unrighteousness is involved, there is nothing we can do to prevent death or forestall it when the appointed time has come. We should leave the burden of such groundless guilt at the feet of the Savior and "bear a song away," focusing on past joys and lessons learned rather than on facts we cannot and need not change.[88]

MOVING BEYOND REGRET

In this very helpful quote, there are many important ideas for us to consider at the time of the passing of a loved one. Although we might feel that we could have done more to help the loved one, as for death's timing, there is little or nothing we can do, if the appointed time for death has come. So we need not, punish ourselves or feel regret at the passing, provided as Elder Hales has said, that there is no unrighteousness involved.

Even those who have had a so-called "perfect" relationship, have had adjustments, have had squabbles, have had unhappiness, sometimes disagreements—these things are all part of mortality and, if we are overly sensitive at the time of the passing of a loved one, we can harbor some regret. I believe that the loved one who has passed away

---

88   Ibid., page 409.

holds little or no concern over regrets that we may feel and for our own mental health, we should go beyond them as soon as possible.

One regret, as noted above, that is quite common is that when a loved one passes away, for whatever reason, we may not have been by the bedside, or with him or her, such as in an accident that claims the life of a loved one. Again, these are situations that are often beyond our control. And although we might say, what might have been, we may feel some sense of guilt.

All of this suggests that we are living in an imperfect world, we are imperfect beings, who make mistakes all of the time—not that we want to but because we are imperfect. Having said this, however, does not excuse us from continuing to improve, trying to perfect the mistakes we often make, becoming better people. After all, this is what we have come to earth to do and even though we strive for perfection in our lives, we fall short in many ways. So by nature, we have reason to carry with us regrets.

As the hymn suggests at the beginning of this chapter, life is all about improvement and progression. So even though we make mistakes, great or small, we must move forward, trying to do better, realizing that we are in a fallen state, trying our best to be more and more like our Savior.

We must not punish ourselves over our mortal foibles. We simply must keep trying to improve our lives, trying to be better than, as Elder Hales has said, we were the day before. Robert L. Millet encourages us in our effort to improve our lives with these words:

> . . . Elder McConkie delivered an address at Brigham Young University in which he identified as one of the "seven deadly heresies" the idea that we must be perfect in order to be saved. "If we keep two principles in mind," he observed, "we will thereby know that good and faithful members of the Church will be saved even though they are far from perfect in this life. These two principles are (1) that this life is the appointed time for men to prepare to meet God—this life is the day of our probation; and (2) that the same spirit which possesses our bodies at the time we go out of this mortal life shall have power to possess our bodies in that eternal world.

"What we are doing as members of the Church is charting a course leading to eternal life. There was only one perfect being, the Lord Jesus Christ. If men had to be perfect and live all of the law strictly, wholly, and completely, there would be one saved person in eternity. The prophet [Joseph Smith] taught that there are many things to be done, even beyond the grave, in working out our salvation.

And so what we do in this life is chart a course leading to eternal life. That course begins here and now and continues in the realms ahead. We must determine in our hearts and in our souls, with all the power and ability we have, that from this time forward we will press on in righteousness; by so doing we can go where God and Christ are. If we make that firm determination, and are in the course of our duty when this life is over, we will continue in that course in eternity." [89]

THE SAVIOR'S ATONING SACRIFICE COVERS THE TRANSGRESSIONS OF ALL

As we have explained in many places in this book, the atoning sacrifice of our Savior covers both the living and the dead—those who have passed to the other side of the veil and those of us who remain behind. In truth, the atoning sacrifice covers regrets and guilt and remorse and all other mortal concerns and worries.

The "good part" of the gospel and, indeed, of all history is the Savior and his atoning sacrifice. The Atonement of Jesus Christ outweighs, surpasses, and transcends every other mortal event, every new discovery, and every acquisition of knowledge, for without the Atonement all else in life is meaningless.[90]

Brother Callister goes on to say:

The prophets have long testified of the Savior's infinite, suffering nature. Years before his birth, Isaiah declared, "Surely he

89   Millet, Robert L., (1995). Within Reach, Salt Lake City, Utah: Deseret Book Company, pages 16-17.
90   Callister, Tad R (2000). The Infinite Atonement, Salt Lake City, Utah: Deseret Book Company, page 4.

hath borne our griefs, and carried our sorrows"(Isaiah 53:4), and later "in all their affliction he was afflicted" (Isaiah 63:9); see also D&C 133:53). Alma understood the extent of the Savior's descent when he observed, "He shall go forth, suffering pains and afflictions and temptations of every kind; and this that the word might be fulfilled which saith he will take upon him the pains and the sicknesses of his people" (Alma 7:11).[91]

It should go without saying that the Atonement was so all encompassing, so completely comprehensive, so infinite that our pains, both the major ones and also the minor ones such as regret, remorse, and feelings of guilt at the passing of a loved one, are completely covered. This wonderful blessing allows us to put aside these things and move forward with a feeling of peace in our hearts.

MAIN POINTS DISCUSSED IN CHAPTER TWELVE

1. We all are born with foibles and weaknesses; surely we are not perfect beings.

2. Since we are not perfect, in the rough and tumble of life, we sometimes offend—here a careless word, there an unkind thought.

3. Sometimes, even when a partner—husband or wife—is ill or perhaps in a terminal way, we still may inadvertently offend or express exasperation, or impatience. This may be true before an accident at which time a loved-one is killed.

4. All of our imperfections at the time of the passing of a loved-one may lead to regrets.

5. It is very important that we move beyond the regrets, learn from our mistakes, and become better people.

91   Ibid., page 105

Chapter Thirteen
At the passing of a loved one, gratitude should fill our souls

Brethren, shall we not go on in so great a cause? Go forward and not backward. Courage, brethren; and on, on to the victory! Let your hearts rejoice, and be exceedingly glad. Let the earth break forth into singing. Let the dead speak forth anthems of eternal praise to the King Immanuel, who hath ordained, before the world was, that which would enable us to redeem them out of their prison; for the prisoners shall go free.

Let the mountains shout for joy, and all ye valleys cry aloud; and all ye seas and dry lands tell the wonders of your Eternal King! And ye rivers, and brooks, and rills, flow down with gladness. Let the woods and all the trees of the field praise the Lord; and ye solid rocks weep for joy! And let the sun, moon, and the morning stars sing together, and let all the sons of God shout for joy! And let the eternal creations declare his name forever and ever! And again I say, how glorious is the voice we hear from heaven, proclaiming in our ears, glory, and salvations, and honor, and immortality, and eternal life; kingdoms, principalities, and powers! [92]

In this chapter, I will focus a few pages on those doctrinal truths which bring great comfort to our hearts and minds for which we will be ever grateful, especially at the passing of a loved one.

SINCERE GRATITUDE IS A BEAUTIFUL THING

There are few places in scripture which capture the exceeding beauty and wonder of the Restoration of the Gospel of Jesus Christ as we find in the verses quoted on the previous page (See D&C 128:22-23). Indeed, these are some of the most beautiful expressions of gratitude ever written:

> "Let the earth break forth into singing; Let the dead speak forth anthems of eternal praise to the King Immanuel; Let the mountains shout for joy, and all ye valleys cry aloud; and all ye seas and dry lands tell the wonders of your Eternal King!; And let the sun, moon, and the morning stars sing together; etc.."

Few words in all of scripture are as touching—they fill our hearts with gratitude! How exciting it is to be a part of this great latter-day work; how exciting it is to know that the heavens are once again open; how wonderful to have a "voice of gladness for the living and the dead;" how humbling it is to have membership in the only true Church; what a profound blessing it is to be led by prophets and apostles in these troubled days; what a magnificent privilege it is to be on the earth in this dispensation. Indeed, let "the mountains shout for joy" at the myriad blessings we enjoy as faithful members of the Church.

And at the passing of a loved one, we ought to be all the more grateful for the Plan of Salvation and Happiness authored by our Heavenly Father and for the redeeming blood of our Savior Jesus Christ which make our progress toward eternity possible. Knowing these things, the passing of a loved one, although cause for mourning and sorrow for a time, brings a feeling of great gratitude into our hearts for the knowledge we have as faithful Latter-day Saints of what the future holds for each of us.

> As we travel through this topsy-turvy, sinful world, filled with temptations and problems, we are humbled by the expectancy of death, the uncertainty of life, and the power and love of God. Sadness comes to all of us in the loss of loved ones. But there is gratitude also. Gratitude for the assurance we have that life is eternal. Gratitude for the great gospel plan, given freely to all of us. Gratitude for the life, teachings, and sacrifice of the Lord Jesus Christ.[93]

---

93   Benson, Ezra Taft (1988). The Teachings of Ezra Taft Benson, Salt Lake City, Utah: Bookcraft, page 364.

In this wonderful quote, President Benson brings great comfort to all of us as we face the death of a loved one—of course there is sorrow and sadness, of course we mourn the passing of a loved one—but at those times especially, we should find in our hearts a sense of gratitude for the great Plan of Salvation and for the atoning sacrifice of our Lord and Savior Jesus Christ. It is through the great plan and the atoning sacrifice that we have a clear picture of the future and for that we should be very grateful. And thus, at the passing of a loved one, we find a place in our hearts for rejoicing and singing praises to a loving Heavenly Father who is the author of the wondrous plan of hope.

THE PEOPLE OF AMMON WERE FILLED WITH GRATITUDE

There are many poignant stories of great sadness and hardship in the holy scriptures with attendant gratitude. Let me refer to the story of the people of Ammon in Alma 24 of the Book of Mormon. In this story, we have converted Lamanites through the teaching of Ammon and his brethren. Many thousands of these people repented of their sins and accepted the Gospel and then they wanted to bury their "weapons of war" as a sign of their humility and gratitude before God. They knew, if they did bury their weapons, that the unconverted Lamanites would no doubt come upon them in an attempt to destroy them. But they were undaunted in their determination to show before God their willingness to completely repent of past iniquities including murder.

With this as background, their king, Anti-Nephi-Lehi, gave a touching and tearful speech to his people. I quote just four verses here from Alma 24, verses 7-10 to help us capture the sense of gratitude which the king expressed to the people:

> . . . I thank my God, my beloved people, that our great God has in goodness sent these our brethren, the Nephites, unto us to preach unto us, and to convince us of the traditions of our wicked fathers.

> And behold, I thank my great God that he has given us a portion of his Spirit to soften our hearts, that we have opened a correspondence with these brethren, the Nephites.

> And behold, I also thank my God, that by opening this cor-
> respondence we have been convinced of our sins, and of the many
> murders which we have committed.

> And I also thank my God, yea, my great God, that he hath
> granted unto us that we might repent of these things, and also that
> he hath forgiven us of those our many sins and murders which
> we have committed, and taken away the guilt from our hearts,
> through the merits of his Son.

It is difficult to imagine the humility, the sincere gratitude of these people. They all knew the implications of their commitment to bury their weapons of war; the mothers especially knew what may result for them and for their children. Shortly after, of course, the unconverted Lamanites came upon them and killed a thousand and five of these unresisting Saints who knelt down before their enemies and died with repentant and grateful hearts.

> And thus we see that, when these Lamanites were brought to
> believe and to know the truth, they were firm, and would suffer
> even unto death rather than commit sin; and thus we see that they
> buried their weapons of peace, or they buried the weapons of war,
> for peace (verse 19).

DEVELOPING A SENSE OF GRATITUDE

For those of us who have had loved ones pass away, we can learn a sobering lesson about gratitude from this story. In short, our adherence to and our gratitude for the Gospel of Jesus Christ and to the great Plan of Salvation transcends even the death of loved ones!

Our expressions of gratitude should be a part of our daily prayers, obviously. We should be filled with gratitude for all we have as members of the Church. We cannot be lazy or forgetful in thanking a condescending God for all that we have. At the same time, we don't want to neglect thanking those around us. For, if we do, just as we may displease our Heavenly Father if we don't express our gratitude to Him, we may disappoint those to whom we owe so much, such as parents, friends, and other loved ones. And not only that, we may disappoint ourselves for words of gratitude not expressed and end up feeling some remorse for thanks not uttered.

Sometimes, before or after the death of a loved one, we may feel some regret that we haven't been more grateful or that we haven't expressed appreciation sufficiently to a loved one. President Howard W. Hunter tells a story which has something to do with regret, but also much to do with gratitude. He says:

> Some time ago I had a lesson of gratitude taught to me. I was in the mission home in San Francisco when the mission president received a telephone call and said, "I must cross the bay and take a message to an elder that his father has just passed away" I went with him. We crossed over the Bay Bridge, up to Berkeley, and stopped at an apartment building. A fine looking elder came to the door. He was excited to see his mission president and said, "Oh, president, come in; we want to tell you what happened this morning." The president said, "Elder, sit down with us for a moment; we have a sad message to deliver to you."
>
> I will never forget that occasion as the young man's head fell into his arms and he commenced to sob. After we had comforted him he said, "My father was the greatest man I have ever known. I have never told him that. I don't believe I realized it in my years of growing up, but since I have come into the mission field a maturity has come to me to make me appreciate my father and my mother. I decided last week I was going to sit down and write my father a letter and tell him how much I loved him and how much he has meant to me, but now it is too late." He commenced to sob again.[94]

My heart went out to that young man, but I thought how typical that is of many of us. The letter we intended to write, the word of appreciation we intended to express to the Lord our appreciation for his goodness. We are grateful for all of these things that are done for us, of course, but in our busy life we don't always express appreciation for what others do for us.

---

94   Williams Clyde J., (editor) (2002). The Teachings of Howard W. Hunter, Salt Lake City, Utah:Deseret Book Company, page 94

In addition to missed opportunities to express our gratitude to people we love, we are sometimes, for whatever reason, downright forgetful to express gratitude. And not only that, we sometimes are even ungrateful.

Truman Madsen tells a humorous anecdote about ingratitude under the title of "Invincible Ingratitude."

> At the top of a steep hill a man was cutting his lawn. In the corner of his eye he saw a lad facing down the sidewalk on a wagon. The next time he looked with horror. The lad was hurtling downward oblivious to the death-dealing freeway below.
>
> The man raced toward the wagon, then realized he could only catch it by a desperate leap. One hand caught on, but then he was dragged and scraped. The wagon finally stopped. The lad turned to his bleeding and bruised benefactor, "Hey, mister, get your hands off my wagon!"

Brother Madsen, using scripture, then helps us understand the spirit of gratitude. He says:

> "For what doth it profit a man if a gift is bestowed upon him and he receive not the gift? Behold, he rejoices not in that which is given unto him, neither rejoices in him who is the giver of the gift" (D&C 88:33).
>
> We can only enjoy that which we are willing to receive
>
> Christ has been and is involved in our lives, and he makes diving leaps in our behalf. We may be asleep to him, indifferent to him, even callously opposed to him. Yet he has promised that those who receive him will receive more abundantly, "even power" (D&C 71:6). He has promised that this abundance will be multiplied through the manifestations of his Spirit (D&C 70:13).
>
> "For whosoever hath, to him shall be given, and he shall have more abundance; but whosoever hath not, from him shall be taken away even that he hath" (Matthew 13:12).

"The great misery of departed spirits in the world of spirits, where they go after death, is to know that they come short of the glory that others enjoy and that they might have enjoyed themselves, and they are their own accusers." (Note: this last sentence is attributed to Joseph Smith, June 11, 1843: see <ins>History of the Church</ins> 5:425)[95]

We understand the spirit of what the Prophet Joseph Smith has said in the last sentence above. In one sense, we will all likely have some regret that we weren't more grateful to the Lord and to other people as we move through mortality.

THE FAMILIAR STORY OF THE CLEANSED TEN LEPERS

There is much to learn from Luke who tells the familiar story of the ten lepers who the Savior cleansed of leprosy:

And it came to pass, as he went to Jerusalem, that he passed through the midst of Samaria and Galilee.

And as he entered into a certain village, there met him ten men that were lepers, which stood afar off;

And they lifted up their voices, and said, Jesus, Master, have mercy on us.

And when he saw them, he said unto them, Go shew yourselves unto the priests. And it came to pass that, as they went, they were cleansed.

And one of them, when he saw that he was healed, turned back, and with a loud voice glorified God.

And fell down on his face at his feet, giving him thanks; and he was a Samaritan.

95   Madsen, Truman G.(2008). <ins>The Sacrament: Feasting at the Lord's Table</ins>, Provo, Utah: Amalphi Publishing, page 56.

And Jesus answering said, Were there not ten cleansed? But where are the nine?

There are not found that returned to give glory to God, save this stranger.

And he said unto him, Arise, go thy way; thy faith hath made thee whole.

All of this is to say that we ought to try all the days of our lives to express appreciation to people around us for their kindnesses and help which they render to us. And it is especially important to express our appreciation to those who are closest to us because not only is it the right thing to do, but we never know when a loved one may be taken from us in a moment, even in a twinkling of an eye. We must not forget to be generous with our words of gratitude. Blessed is the man or woman who watches a lifelong spouse waste away in illness and during that time has opportunity to express love and appreciation to him or her.

CARING FOR A SICK LOVED ONE IS OFTENTIMES DIFFICULT

Let me add that many times during an extended illness prior to death, there is much about caring for a loved one that is difficult. There may be many hours sitting by a loved one's side and the accompanying fatigue; there is the constant providing of nourishment, providing drinks of water, and other necessities that even require going down to the neighborhood store "for the hundredth time" to purchase something that may provide comfort for the loved one. There are on-going doctor's appointments to meet; there is the fear that the next test result may be a grim assessment of his or her condition.

And then too there is much about caring for a very ill and dying person that is distasteful—there may be a spilled glass of juice which fell from a shaky hand; there may be sheets that must be changed, sometimes even on a daily basis; there may be smells that are potentially embarrassing to the loved one. All of these things require much patience.

Imagine though, that all through these experiences there is a constant stream of "thank you's" and not just from the patient, but from the care giver—thank you for our wonderful life together; thank you for all the times that you cared for me; thank you for your good life which has brought much happiness to me; thank you for your faithfulness in the Gospel; thank you for loving our children and being such a good father or mother; thank you for being patient with me when I wasn't at my best; thank you for forgiving my foolishness on so many occasions, etc., etc.

These tender words of gratitude won't change the course of the inevitable death, but they will bring so much comfort to both the one who is slipping away and the one who is helping in the hours of need.

These are tender and sad times, but they are made so much better when there are grateful hearts involved.

President Monson and Elder Hales summarize nicely the spirit of gratitude which can be applied easily to our discussion of death and dying:

> President Thomas S. Monson spoke of the power of gratitude when he stated, "We can lift ourselves and others as well when we refuse to remain in the realm of negativity thought and cultivate within our hearts an attitude of gratitude." And Elder Robert D. Hales of the Quorum of the Twelve Apostles has suggested that "in some quiet way, the expression and feelings of gratitude have a wonderful cleansing or healing nature . . . Gratitude brings a peace that helps us overcome the pain of adversity and failure." Truly, following the words of prophets to live with a sense of gratitude invites a spirit of happiness into our lives.

MAIN POINTS DISCUSSED
IN CHAPTER THIRTEEN

1. We are a very blessed people—we have membership in the true Church; we have an understanding of the great Plan of Salvation; and

we have a Savior who has redeemed us from the effects of the Fall of Adam.

2. With all these blessings, we ought to be a grateful people, especially at the passing of a loved one.

3. During our association with family members, we should be especially expressive of our gratitude since we never know when they might be called to pass through the veil.

Chapter Fourteen
Is there anything I've done to you for which I should apologize?

> Wherefore, I say unto you, that ye ought to forgive one another; for he that forgiveth not his brother his trespasses standeth condemned before the Lord; for there remaineth in him the greater sin.
>
> I, the Lord, will forgive whom I will forgive, but of you it is required to forgive all men.
>
> Doctrine and Covenants 64:9-10

I worked with a colleague, Dr. Dillon Inouye, for a number of years at Brigham Young University who was a brilliant and thoughtful scholar, who often came forward with wonderful ideas and suggestions to improve the program in which we were engaged. One day, he came to me, after he had had a "restless night" and asked,

> "Wayne, you and I have worked together for a long time. I know in the rough and tumble of life there are always things that we do that may offend others. So, I'm asking, is there anything I should apologize for?"

I was so impressed at his thoughtful concern that our relationship be preserved that he was willing to humble himself (a characteristic not common in the university community) and ask forgiveness for something he had perhaps unwittingly done. Imagine how I was affected by this humble and brilliant man. To this day, long after my friend has passed away, I think of this lesson and try to do the same!

In my view, forgiveness is the key ingredient in our relationships with spouses, with children, with neighbors and friends. It is a requirement placed upon us to forgive! In truth, this is the magic ingredient for successful relationships before and after someone we love has passed away.

Forgiveness is one of those responsibilities we have by way of commandment from the Lord Himself throughout our entire lives. He reminds us often in the scriptures to forgive one another. This is one of those requirements like gratitude we should be developing all through our lives and not just at the time of the death of a loved one although it surely should be carefully refined when a loved one does pass away.

From the Book of Mosiah 26:29-31, we read:

> . . . and if he confess his sins before thee and me, and repenteth in the sincerity of his heart, him shall ye forgive, and I will forgive him also.

> Yea, and as often as my people repent will I forgive them their trespasses against me.

> And ye shall also forgive one another your trespasses; for verily I say unto you, he that forgiveth not his neighbor's trespasses when he says that he repents, the same hath brought himself under condemnation.

And again we read from 3rd Nephi 13:14-15:

> For, if ye forgive men their trespasses your heavenly Father will also forgive you;

> But if ye forgive not men their trespasses neither will your Father forgive your trespasses.

I'm reminded of an experience I had many years ago while discussing with a friend a number of verses from Doctrine and Covenants 98:38-48 which pertain to forgiveness. Let me first quote the scripture (which is quite long) and then give the wonderful lesson I received from my friend.

> Behold, this is an ensample unto all people, saith the Lord your God, for justification before me.

And again, verily I say unto you, if after thine enemy has come upon thee the first time, he repent and come unto thee praying thy forgiveness, thou shalt forgive him, and shalt hold it no more as a testimony against thine enemy—

And so on unto the second and third time; and as oft as thine enemy repenteth of the trespass wherewith he has trespassed against thee, thou shalt forgive him, until seventy times seven.

And if he trespass against thee and repent not the first time, nevertheless thou shalt forgive him.

And if he trespass against thee the second time, and repent not, nevertheless thou shalt forgive him.

And if he trespass against thee the third time, and repent not, thou shalt also forgive him.

But if he trespass against thee the fourth time thou shalt not forgive him, but shalt bring these testimonies before the Lord; and they shall not be blotted out until he repent and reward thee fourfold in all things wherewith he has trespassed against thee.

And if he do this, thou shalt forgive him with all thine heart; and if he do not this, I, the Lord, will avenge thee of thine enemy an hundred-fold;

And upon his children, and upon his children's children of all them that hate me, unto the third and fourth generation.

But if the children repent, or the children's children, and turn to the Lord their God, with all their hearts and with all their might, mind and strength, and restore four-fold for all their trespasses wherewith they have trespassed, or wherewith their fathers have trespassed, or their father's fathers, then thine indignation shall be turned away;

And vengeance shall no more come upon them, saith the Lord
thy God, and their trespasses shall never be brought any more as a
testimony before the Lord against them. Amen.

My friend, knowing of this section in the Doctrine and Covenants,
then told of a situation with which he was closely involved. Apparently
there were two Latter-day Saint friends who started a business many,
many decades before. After some time, the business began to fail, then
completely collapsed. These friends, because of the failed business, became bitter enemies each claiming that the other "cheated" in their
business dealings. They both went to their graves not having resolved
the matter.

A grandson of one of these men learned about this situation and
began to collect all possible information he could find about it. He discovered, to the best of his knowledge, that although somewhat fuzzy, it
was his own grandfather who had cheated and knew exactly how much
money was involved.

He immediately went to work, saved a large sum of money, in
truth, four times the amount which was involved in the sour business
dealing.

He then went to the grandson of the other partner and paid him,
in a spirit of humility, four times the amount owing. At first the other
grandson was unwilling to accept the money—"It happened long ago!"
But the other grandson insisted for the blessing of his own family and
his grandfather's "children's children" until his own generation; and for
his grandfather's sake who now needs to be forgiven of his trespass.

All of this is to suggest that before and after the passing of a loved
one, our hearts should be "right" and filled with the spirit of forgiveness.
Obviously, there is much for which we all need to seek forgiveness—it's
the way mortality is set up—we have to deal with our own selfishness,
our own weaknesses and do the best we can to overcome them.

As I've noted before in this book, the loved one who has passed
away will have quickly moved forward doing what is required in the
world of the Spirits. He or she will have long ago forgiven us. But it is
for us here, to forgive for whatever trespasses our loved one may have

trespassed against us. It is surely not good for our souls to harbor any lasting trespasses.

In our quiet moments of prayer after our loved one has passed through the veil, we need to beg Heavenly Father for forgiveness of any trespass which we have inflicted upon that loved one, and perhaps those trespasses the loved one has inflicted upon us. Then we move on!

REPENTANCE IS THE GATEWAY TO FORGIVENESS

It is the genuine spirit of repentance that makes forgiveness possible. Indeed, it is the precursor to forgiveness. President Spencer W. Kimball declared that repentance is "the gateway to forgiveness."[96] So when we contemplate the loss of a loved one, and whereas it is often too late to make full amends with a spouse, for example, at death's door, we can after the passing make those amends through repentance with the assurance that we will receive forgiveness. This is, of course, the great miracle—that we can be forgiven of any sin or transgression—of the great kind or of the lesser, even the foolish and the thoughtless kind—the kind that we sometimes regret after the passing of a loved one.

The miracle of forgiveness is wonderful in that we will have the assurance, if we forgive any trespass of a departed loved one, that he or she will forgive us also. Now it would obviously be better to have all these things sorted out before death, but knowing our frailties and our imperfections, many minor or even major transgressions aren't resolved between the departed one and those who remain behind before death's caskets are opened and closed. But no matter, all can be resolved, either on this side of the veil or on the other side.

President Kimball continues to help us. He says:

> The essence of the miracle of forgiveness is that it brings peace to the previously anxious, restless, frustrated, perhaps tormented soul. In a world of turmoil and contention this is indeed a priceless gift.[97]

96   Kimball, Spencer W. (1969). <u>The Miracle of Forgiveness</u>, Salt Lake City, Utah: Bookcraft, Inc., page 14.

97   <u>Ibid</u>., page 363

He goes on to say:

> Peace is the fruit of righteousness. It cannot be bought with
> money, and cannot be traded nor bartered. It must be earned. The
> wealthy often spend much of their gains in a bid for peace, only to
> find that it is not for sale. But the poorest as well as the richest may
> have it in abundance if the total price is paid. Those who abide the
> laws and live the Christ-like life may have peace and other kindred
> blessings, principal among which are exaltation and eternal life.[98]

And we must remember what Alma taught in his stirring speech to
those Book of Mormon people living in the land of Gideon. He said
(see Alma 7:25 and 27):

> And may the Lord bless you, and keep your garments spot-
> less, that ye may at last be brought to sit down with Abraham,
> Isaac, and Jacob, and the holy prophets who have been ever since
> the world began, having your garments spotless even as their gar-
> ments are spotless, in the kingdom of heaven to go no more out.

> And now, may the peace of God rest upon you, and upon
> your houses and lands, and upon your flocks and herds, and all
> that you possess, your women and your children, according to
> your faith and good works, from this time forth and forever. And
> thus I have spoken. Amen

We must not live in the past; we must make amends and move on
into the bright sunshine of forgiveness and peace. Two weeks before
my wife died, I learned that a friend's wife also died. Ten months or
so later, we met and talked about our "loss." He was still grieving! He
wondered, because of his imperfections, if she was dissatisfied with
him and would be happier with another man. He was not at peace, the
peace that comes with forgiveness. I tried to explain that, whereas you
both made very minor errors even during the time when she was dying, those errors will be completely subsumed in the love of our Savior
Jesus Christ and His atoning sacrifice. "Your task," I said, "is to forgive
yourself and her, and move forward knowing that both you and she are

---

98   Ibid., page 363-364

forgiven by each other and by the Lord. When this happens, you will be at peace; your heart will be content and calm."

MAIN POINTS DISCUSSED IN CHAPTER FOURTEEN

1. In all our doings with our fellow men, especially with family members, we must carry continually in our hearts the spirit of forgiveness.

2. It is a good thing if before and after the passing of a loved one, we have the spirit of forgiveness in our hearts.

3. It is in forgiveness that our hearts will be calm and at peace at the passing of a loved one.

4. Repentance is the gateway to forgiveness. If we want to obtain the forgiveness for which we honestly seek, it will come through sincere and humble repentance.

5. The future for the humble and repentant person is not only to receive forgiveness but also to have the assurance of eternal life with the loved one who has moved ahead on progression's path.

6. In the rough and tumble of life, we may offend someone dear to us. It is because of this that we should reach out and seek forgiveness from those around us, especially the ones who are closest to us in our circle of love.

Chapter Fifteen
Obituaries: What do we want written of us after we pass through the veil?

And when she passed I think there went a soul to yonder firmament so white, so splendid and so fine it came complete to God's design.

Edgar Guest

Obituaries represent an official pronouncement of the deceased loved one as he or she leaves mortality; it is a record to be preserved by the family which can be reviewed from time to time. It is a written expression which should reflect the desires of the deceased loved one; perhaps the things accomplished in mortality; and most especially their love for the Lord and His Gospel. We surely want to express in the obituary what the loved one would say, knowing that he or she is viewing things on the other side of the veil from a very different perspective. The obituary should also serve as a comfort to all who read it; and it should be an inspiration, helping all of us to be better people. In all cases, we will want the obituary to please the loved one who has passed on to the eternities.

In addition to these expressions, one friend suggested to me recently that faithful saints may want to consider emphasizing missionary work when writing an obituary. His reasoning, and I concur, is that faithful Latter-day Saints, when they pass through the veil, will hit the ground running so to speak pertaining to missionary work. After all that is what our Savior spends His time doing in the Spirit World—organizing his faithful servants so that they can go about preaching the Gospel to all spirits in that world. As we see in D&C 138:30-32:

But behold, from among the righteous, he organized his forces and appointed messengers, clothed with power and authority, and commissioned them to go forth and carry the light of the gospel to them that were in darkness, even to all the spirits of men; and thus was the gospel preached to the dead.

And the chosen messengers went forth to declare the acceptable day of the Lord and proclaim liberty to the captives who were bound, even unto all who would repent of their sins and receive the gospel.

Thus was the gospel preached to those who had died in their sins, without a knowledge of the truth, or in transgression, having rejected the prophets.

It probably is a good idea to remember what faithful Latter-day Saints will be doing on the other side of the veil. And that, of course, is to preach the Gospel to those in the world of Spirits who haven't had an opportunity to hear it while they were in our mortal estate.

It is well for others, perhaps the less active or even non-members to know what is going on in the world of Spirits. It may be a motivation for them to bring their lives into full compliance with Gospel teachings. Indeed, many folks will read the obituary and be influenced by it; or equally important, non-Latter-day Saints may read it and be influence by it to investigate the Church. This would, obviously, bring a loud cheer from the deceased!

In some cases, the obituary could be a potential embarrassment to deceased persons for the second they passed through the veil, their perspective on mortality changes dramatically—they realize that their commitment to the Gospel of Jesus Christ is all important, not earthly achievement. So when preparing an obituary, we might want to remember where they are and what is most important to them now that they are in the Spirit World.

WHAT THINKS CHRIST OF ME?

When a loved one passes to the other side of the veil, as we've spoken repeatedly in this book, it should be a time of rejoicing and happiness if, and it's a big if, he or she has been true and faithful to the Restored Gospel of Jesus Christ. The true disciples of Christ want to be remem-

bered for their faith, courage, and diligence in keeping the commandments. These sorts of things far outweigh any worldly accomplishment.
Accordingly, I believe the obituary should reflect what faithful people
think about Jesus; their love for Him; and their commitment to Him.
These things, when you think about it, you will want included in your
own obituary and in the obituaries of those you love.

In an inspirational speech given in the 2012 April General Conference, Elder Neil L. Andersen made a number of important points that
will be helpful as we write obituaries for our loved ones, and as our
loved ones may have to write obituaries for us. He asks us to think of
the question, "What thinks Christ of me?" He also asks, "Does my life
reflect the love and devotion I feel for the Savior." He goes on to say,

> In the final assessment, our personal discipleship will not be
> judged by friends or foes. Rather, as Paul said, "We shall all stand
> before the judgment seat of Christ" (Romans 14:10). At that day
> the important question for each of us will be, "What thinks Christ
> of me?"[99]

The question, "Does my life reflect the love and devotion I feel for
the Savior" is the very key, in my judgment, to writing an obituary.
With this key question in mind, we might ask, "Does the obituary
reflect the love and devotion I feel for the Savior?" If so, the words written will make for a perfect obituary! Knowing what the future holds in
terms of our standing before Christ at His judgment bar, would we not
want to present in the obituary our devotion?

WHAT DO DISCIPLES OF CHRIST WANT TO EXPRESS TO THE WORLD?

With these thoughts in mind, we might want to consider reflecting
on what discipleship has meant to the deceased loved one. Although
not present, "What is it that the deceased loved one would want to
share with the world? We know that worldly accomplishments aren't
going to impress many people especially those on the other side of
the veil and they won't impress many people on this side. So why not

---

99   Ensign Magazine, May 2012, page 111

write the obituary trying to reflect the meaning and value of his or her discipleship?

Of course, in our obituary we want people to think well of us, even though we may have had many blemishes in our life as we journeyed in mortality. What is important is that we declare, especially in the obituary the joy the deceased experienced in life as a disciple of Christ. No one is perfect but what is important that they have gone beyond mortal transgressions and sins and are now prepared to offer to the Lord a broken heart and contrite spirit.

We cannot forget that what we want to present to the Lord, as we hope will be reflected in our obituary, is that we lived our lives in mortality with a broken heart and a contrite spirit. Jesus taught the Nephites (see 3 Nephi 9:19-20:

> And ye shall offer up unto me no more the shedding of blood; yea, your sacrifices and your burnt offerings shall be done away, for I will accept none of your sacrifices and your burnt offerings.
>
> And ye shall offer for a sacrifice unto me a broken heart and a contrite spirit. And whoso cometh unto me with a broken heart and a contrite spirit, him will I baptize with fire and with the Holy Ghost, even as the Lamanites, because of their faith in me at the time of their conversion, were baptized with fire and with the Holy Ghost . . .

WORLDLY ACCOMPLISHMENTS ARE OF LITTLE IMPORT TO JESUS

Focusing the obituary on worldly accomplishments should be carefully considered. More appropriate would be to focus attention on testimony, upon service in the mission field; service to his fellow human beings. These sorts of things far outweigh worldly accomplishments, especially the accomplishment of accruing wealth. Anything in the obituary which reflects wealth should be carefully considered, especially in light of scriptural injunctions like the following:

> And again I say unto you, It is easier for a camel to go through
> the eye of a needle, than for a rich man to enter into the kingdom
> of God (Matthew 19:24).

S. Michael Wilcox reminds us of many important teachings about prosperity and raises difficult questions which should help us put wealth in its proper perspective. He says:

> ... I understand that wealth, riches, and affluence are relative
> terms, so it might be helpful to begin with a definition. The best I
> have come across is one offered by President Spencer W. Kimball,
> commenting on Matthew 19:24. He wrote, "We may say that he
> is rich whose accumulations are sufficiently great to blind him to
> his spiritual and moral obligations and to render him slave instead
> of master."[100]

While on the subject of wealth and the writing of obituaries, Brother Wilcox provides for us a powerful and insightful Buddhist parable which we should keep in mind when considering riches. Here's the parable:

> A number of children are playing on the shore building sand
> castles. Each thinks his or hers is the finest, and they all defend
> their portion of shoreline, beach sand, and what they have cre-
> ated out of it with vigor, saying, "This one is mine!" They keep
> their castles separate and apart, frequently comparing theirs with
> the other children's handiwork. In their own minds, there is never
> any question about which territory or which castle belongs to any
> individual child. All are sure of their proprietary ownership. All
> are building feverishly. Occasionally, there are quarrels when one
> child kicks over another child's castle. Then, enraged, the owner
> retaliates, sometimes with the support of other children. And so
> the day wears on, each child enlarging or improving or changing
> his castle according to his whims and wishes. "This is mine! No
> one else may have it! Keep away! Don't touch my castle!" they
> cry to each other. In time the day draws to a close, and evening
> descends upon the playing children. As it gets dark, the children
> decide they have played enough and it is time to go home. No

100   Wilcox, S. Michael (2010) What the Scriptures Teach Us about Prosperity, Salt Lake
City, Utah: Deseret Book, page 1.

one now cares about their castles. They turn their faces from the shore and walk away, leaving their creations to the wind and the rising tide.[101]

Brother Wilcox concludes this "tiny parable" with the following:

> If Elder Melvin J. Ballard is right—and I firmly believe he is—then the turning away as the sun sets on the shore for the Latter-day Saints will not be difficult. Let the world squabble over the height or splendor or their castles. We are preparing for mansions on high built by the Savior himself, which we will inherit because we have passed through the needle's eye.

THE OBITUARY: SHOULD BE TRUE TO DOCTRINES OF THE RESTORATION AND BE FAITH PROMOTING

Based on what has been said above, it seems to me to be important to consider the doctrines associated with the death of a loved one. It is the doctrine which has been emphasized in this book because it is reflective of what is important for all of us in mortality. And yet, as I study obituaries, there appears to be so much said that doesn't reflect the doctrines which have come to us in the Restored Gospel of Jesus Christ. For when you think about it, what else is as important as the doctrines of the Kingdom of God and the commandments which God the Father has put upon us? Think about Joseph Smith's funeral addresses, very little is even mentioned about the worldly accomplishments of the deceased, as for example, in his King Follett funeral speech. He's surely not interested in extolling the virtues of deceased persons pertaining to worldly accomplishments, but much more interested in their faithfulness; their commitment to the Gospel; their obedience to commandments; their Church service. And why is this so? It is so because the only really important thing for us in mortality is to be honorable in keeping the commandments. That's all there is about mortality that is important, not aspiring to the honors of men which, if achieved, are nice but not really important in the eternal scope of things.

---

101   Ibid., pages 188-189.

At the passing of a loved one, we want to be sure, when we write the obituary (our own or a loved one) that we consider two things: The first is that we focus on the doctrines which are fundamental to life and death as they have been outlined in this book. The second is, we surely will want to keep in mind that what is written reflects what is important for people to read and hear about us or our loved one who has passed away that will build their faith in the Restored Gospel of Jesus Christ. If we keep these things in mind, the obituaries we do write will be a source of satisfaction for us on this side of the veil, and pleasing to those who have passed to the other side.

And we'll want to reflect in the obituary truth, that is true doctrine. Unfortunately, we read all the time print that is questionable. For example, we read every day in the newspaper expressions like, "B. . . has returned to his Heavenly Father . . ." or "B . . . is now wrapped in the arms of a loving Father in Heaven." Well, if the people who wrote the obituary mean Heavenly Father (Elohim), that's simply false doctrine. If they mean Jesus Christ, whose children we are, it may not be that Jesus will be on the other side welcoming us. Rather He has put into place an organization; we will surely feel His spirit and presence as he directs the work that goes on in the world of spirits. But, we may not necessarily see Him. So getting our doctrine right is important and should be reflected in the written obituary.

The thoughts noted in the above paragraph are sometimes traced to language we find in Alma 40:11 which reads:

> Now, concerning the state of the soul between death and the resurrection—Behold, it has been made known unto me by an angel, that the spirits of all men, as soon as they are departed from this mortal body, yea, the spirits of all men, whether they be good or evil, are taken home to that God who gave them life.

We know that the God who gave us life is Jesus Christ; we are His children as we read in Mosiah 5. So it is important to know this in order that we don't mislead ourselves or others when we present an obituary. We must get the doctrine right!

Because of these and other problems associated with hastily written obituaries, it is as is obvious, that sufficient time needs to be spent on writing a thoughtful and truly reflective obituary, so that you can be assured that what is written is pleasing to the deceased, and to His Savior. As is true with all written documents, especially obituaries, taking the time to write carefully and thoughtfully will prove to honor the loved one who has passed through the veil; and be of great interest and comfort to those who remain on this side of the veil.

TRY TO MAKE THE OBITUARY INTERESTING, READABLE, AND CAPTIVATING

Of all the documents that are written, the obituary is the one that is usually most hastily put together, with only a few days between the death of a person and the funeral unless, of course, the obituary has been written before the death occurs. Two or three days don't give us much time to carefully consider the words that are put to paper. Because of this, most obituaries are sometimes rote, following patterns that are normally printed in local newspapers. And because there are deadlines put on us to meet newspaper and other media requirements, the documents are written hastily and sometimes aren't really the words that the deceased might want said, and may not be doctrinally sound. As for being rote, the language that is often used is usually a standard kind of language that is often misleading or downright inaccurate. For example, many obituaries make a statement something like, "M . . . passed away after a valiant fight with cancer." What does it mean to have a valiant fight against cancer? Does this mean that the person was courageous in the face of death? If so, why not say that? What about saying something like, "M . . . died recently with dignity and courage sharing happy moments with her close family." Here's an example of a thoughtfully considered comment in an obituary written in 2011:

> On July 18th we bid a heartfelt farewell to a special lady. She bravely faced the insidious challenges of A.L.S. (Lou Gehrig's Disease) for almost a year. She died at home with family near.

This kind of language suggests this good sister had courage, but didn't follow the kind of rote language that is often written in the local press. Or think about the wording of the following obituary which was written by the deceased person himself prior to his death:

> I have unbounded gratitude to the Lord, who blessed me with
> a believing heart in early childhood. I have not feared death except
> for twinges of conscience that I could have lived a better life.

The second sentence is very interesting. This person doesn't for a moment fear death except he says, in a humorous way, he has "twinges of conscience" that he could have done better in his life which, obviously, reflects his humility and sense of repentance.

So, being thoughtful and reflective about the deceased and taking the time to write those things that are special will make for a good obituary. All obituaries are special but with time and thought, they can be much more interesting and inspiring than the ones normally found in local newspapers.

THE DECEASED'S GENEALOGY, TEMPLE WORK, AND MISSIONARY WORK SHOULD BE THE POINTS OF EMPHASIS IN A DISCIPLE'S OBITUARY.

In addition to presenting true doctrine in the obituary and providing comfort to the loved ones who remain on this side of the veil, it is also important to consider what missionary mileage the obituary can achieve. This is especially true if the deceased has served a mission either when young or old. Indeed, in the many obituaries I have read, the focus on this great work is most impressive. Describing missionary work, knowing this is the most important work he or she has likely done in life, is impressive and is a manifestation of his or her discipleship.

The same applies to genealogical and temple work. Since Joseph Smith explained that seeking after our kindred dead is the most important work we can do in mortality, when this dimension of a person's life is emphasized in the obituary, it tells volumes about the deceased's discipleship.

We must remember that on the other side of the veil, faithful servants will be engaged primarily in preaching the Gospel and in seeking after kindred dead. These activities will be well organized and ordered. In this sense, all of our lives should be devoted to preparation for the great work that takes place on the other side of the veil. In a real sense, mortality is one big Family History and Temple Preparation class; or we might think of mortality as one big Missionary Training Center. These important activities in mortality will help prepare us for the work we'll be doing on the other side of the veil. Should not such important activities be emphasized in the obituary?

MAIN POINTS DISCUSSED
IN CHAPTER FIFTEEN

1. When a loved one passes through the veil, it should be a time of rejoicing and happiness in the Gospel of Jesus Christ. This joy should likely be reflected in the written obituary.

2. We might want to write the obituary as though the deceased was present and who has a very different perspective as to what is important pertaining to mortality.

3. The obituary should be true to doctrines of the Restoration and be faith promoting.

4. Focusing the obituary on worldly accomplishments should be carefully considered.

5. We should likely consider reflecting on what discipleship has meant to the deceased loved one. Although not present, "What is it that the deceased loved one would want to share with the world?

Chapter Sixteen
Funerals: What do we want said about us after we pass through the veil

How consoling to be mourners when they are called to part with a husband, wife, father, mother, child, or dear relative, to know that, although the earthly tabernacle is laid down and dissolved, they shall rise again to dwell in everlasting burnings in immortal glory, not to sorrow, suffer, or die any more, but they shall be heirs of God and joint heirs with Jesus Christ.

Joseph Smith, Jr.

In the previous chapter regarding obituaries, we considered what the deceased would want **written** about him or her. In this chapter we will consider what deceased loved ones who have departed mortality would like **said** over the pulpit during the funeral. Although somewhat the same, there are marked differences between the written obituary and the words spoken during a funeral. We might consider the obituary a written account of the deceased's life, whereas the funeral is an oral account. In this chapter, I want to present information that may be helpful in planning a spiritual and inspirational funeral.

CONSIDER THE FUNERAL A TIME TO CELEBRATE DISCIPLESHIP

In my view, funerals should be a celebration of a life devoted to the building of the Kingdom of God; of a celebration of one's discipleship both as a member of a family and as a member of the Church. By and large funerals are family affairs and should be seen as a way of emphasizing to family members the deceased's discipleship. If a celebration of discipleship is the focus of a funeral I can assure that the funeral will be both spiritual and inspirational for family members and for all who attend. In truth, when a disciple has passed away, he or she would want to deflect attention on him or her and put it squarely on the Savior and His atoning sacrifice.

Discipleship and family are, for the true and faithful Latter-day Saints, virtually one and the same. On a scale of one to one thousand, at the very top, at the 1000 level is the Gospel of Jesus Christ as it is lived and believed in a family. To devoted disciples, this is the way it has been in their lives. These intertwined things are at the very top of what is important in the lives of the faithful. One friend suggested that Church position could be set at one hundred, considerably down the scale, but very important nonetheless. I suppose worldly accomplishments would settle in around fifty.

From this, we can conclude that discipleship in the context of family should be the main focal point of the funeral. Any other accomplishment would take a back seat to this focus.

Unfortunately, I have observed, having attended many, many funerals in my life that spirituality and inspiration are often lacking in funerals mainly because other things are emphasized rather than discipleship. A funeral devoted to the deceased's discipleship will always draw on doctrine and important truths of the Gospel. And I know that when doctrine and Gospel principles are highlighted during the funeral, everyone is lifted and fulfilled. Without true doctrine presented, what is left is to extol the other virtues of the deceased—the discipleship is downplayed, sometimes entirely overlooked.

I won't repeat here the importance of emphasizing missionary work since that is basically the theme I followed in the previous chapter on obituaries. Disciples are missionaries! They don't want to have other things emphasized during the funeral at the expense of missionary work, or genealogy and temple work.

And I have to say, that on a few occasions, while listening to funeral speeches, had I not known about the life of the deceased, I would not know if they were LDS except for the fact that we were sitting in a LDS chapel. For example, I attended a funeral a number of years ago which was basically a fashion show. Here before the family are the remains of a faithful Latter-day Saint while family members talked almost exclusively of her fashions and jewelry. I kept thinking surely someone would talk Gospel, perhaps read from Alma, or quote from the prophets, but alas, it was not to be. I think it safe to say, that the deceased would not be terribly happy with such talk during her funeral.

Part of the problem lies with the haste with which most funerals are put together. There are many, many arrangements to be made in a very short period of time. And what often happens is that the family members or the loved ones left behind hardly have time to mourn as they scurry around making plans for the funeral. All of this suggests that when possible, careful planning should take place before the final hours so that what is said is, for the most part, what is most important to the deceased.

Then too, the funeral should be seen as a very special, sacred and important event for all the good that it could accomplish. I would hesitate, even though the death of a loved one may be shocking, to turn the arrangements over to someone else not particularly close to the family. This is often done, and often ends in disappointment for obvious reasons.

Then there is the selection of speakers for the funeral. These people should be considered for their ability to discuss discipleship and doctrine in a funeral setting. There are many who could be considered, but one question might be, "Will this person focus attention on the discipleship and doctrine of the Restoration which the deceased loved?"

Even if the deceased had not been true and faithful in his or her days of probation in mortality, the family could still turn the focus to important doctrines and principles of the Gospel. We must remember that the deceased is seeing things in the world of spirits much differently than when in mortality. If the person has been inactive in the Church, from his or her present position, he or she would want to reverse things and pay attention to that which is most important—one's faith in the Lord Jesus Christ.

We don't want to be more than honest here. We don't want to be hypocritical and say things about the deceased which are not true, but with careful thought there are ways to focus attention on the Gospel. Blessed is the family which doesn't have to stretch to make this focus;

in this sense it is easy to make funeral arrangements because what will be planned can easily be taken for granted if the loved one who passes has been strictly faithful.

I have mentioned above the idea of a celebration. What this means is that in the funeral, we can celebrate a faithful discipleship; a faithful father or mother, brother or sister, husband or wife, etc. whose focus of attention throughout life has been first and foremost on the Gospel. Another way to say this is for all of us right now, try to see all of what we do in mortality in the context of the Gospel of Jesus Christ. If that is reflected in the funeral, it will be a superior one and will be a blessing to all who attend. Remember, please, that true doctrine and words about discipleship give the greatest comfort and joy to those who remain behind.

NEEDLESS TO SAY, CAREFUL PLANNING SHOULD BE DONE TO ASSURE A GREAT FUNERAL

So, what are some of the difficulties faced when planning a funeral?

Well, one obvious difficulty is the place where the deceased passes on such as, for example, a different state in the United States, or what is worse if the death occurs in a foreign country. There are always unexpected delays in transferring a body from one state to another, and especially extracting a body from another country. And these transfers are sometimes expensive.

Another difficulty pertains to travel of family members. Sometimes it takes some time for arrangements to be made, especially if they live a great distance from the place where the funeral will be held. Along with this difficulty, is the consideration of who will speak, especially if they have a long distance to travel to get to the funeral; the more time to plan for such eventualities, the better.

Then there are the financial costs associated with funerals. Most people are shocked at the cost of providing a mid-level funeral for a loved one. Depending on a number of considerations, funerals generally begin at around $10,000 and can go much, much higher.

THE COST OF FUNERALS
MAY SHOCK YOU

With all that is said above, I have listed below some of the arrangements[102] and their approximate costs which have to be made for a funeral. In my own case, I was very surprised at the time of the death of a special loved one at how costs had risen dramatically in the last few years. In my case, since the death of a loved one was completely unexpected, and learning of the costs, obviously arrangements for the costs became an important consideration. All of us should be aware of what to expect in terms of cost, especially those who are in their senior years, and who are not that far themselves from departure from mortality. Here is a short listing of some of the expected costs for a mid-level funeral.

1. Basic services of funeral director and staff--$2000

2. Embalming--$685

3. Other preparations of the body such as dressing, casketing, cosmetology, restoration, washing, disinfecting, refrigeration, body donation, hairdresser, plus autopsy—between $1000-$1500.

4. Services and facility fees. These services and fees include: funeral home facilities, funeral home visitations, graveside services, Saturday or Sunday services, Sunday evening visitation or viewing, hourly rate of funeral director—these and related services can amount to more than $3000.

5. Automotive equipment and services: transfer of remains to funeral home, funeral coach, limousine, utility vehicle and driver—these services can amount to about $1000.

Mortuary packages would include most of the above. In selecting these packages, the general cost is as follows:

Church or other facility: $4100

Mortuary Chapel Price: $3700

Graveside service: $3400

---

102   I express appreciation to Spilsbury Mortuary in St. George, Utah for permission to use their funeral arrangement form.

Then we have to consider the cost of caskets (they could range from $1000 to $25,000). Then there are outer burial containers (vaults) which could run from $900 to $11,000. There are also other merchandise costs. You will have to make decisions about flowers, programs, register books, burial clothing, monuments and grave markers which usually cost from $2000 and upward. There are costs for death certificates and transfer permits. If you are planning cremation, there are additional costs for such services.

There are a number of mortuary packages which allow clients to pay for these costs prior to the death of a loved one. Families might want to consider purchasing a tailor-made package that would satisfy their needs.

I have learned that there are some funeral arrangements that could be made with much less cost and it would be good for people, with very limited budgets, to consider such arrangements.

AS IN ALL ELSE WE DO AS FAITHFUL MEMBERS, WE SHOULD FOLLOW THE LEAD OF THE PROPHETS

One important consideration to make at the time of the death of a loved one has to do with length of time for the funeral. Generally speaking, one hour and fifteen minutes to one hour and thirty minutes would be optimal. If not careful, the time can go much longer than the time recommended. I have observed that the funerals of our Church leaders usually follow this time frame.

I have observed another interesting thing at funerals of the prophets and apostles. I see very few tears. I believe there is a relatively easy answer for this. It is that our Church leaders are so confident in and sure about the Plan of Salvation and are so aware of the teachings of other prophets down through the course of history, that there is little reason to shed tears. In truth, the loved one who has passed through the veil has taken a sure step on the path toward eternal life and their lives now are filled with new and exciting experiences, crowned with happiness and joy in living worthy and faithful lives in mortality. There is no need to mourn, as we have read in other places in this book for when a loved one dies, they move on to a very glorious place.

MAIN POINTS DISCUSSED
IN CHAPTER SIXTEEN

1. Obviously, the more time to plan a funeral, knowing of all the decisions that have to be made, the better.

2. Funerals can be a great time of celebration of a good and faithful life.

3. Speaking about discipleship and one's commitment to the Restored Gospel of Jesus Christ always make for the best funerals.

4. There is comfort in the doctrines of the Restored Gospel which suggests that doctrines should be presented in a funeral.

5. We all must realize that there are very high costs associated with a funeral.

6. Since time is often short in planning a funeral, sufficient time should be taken, even while mourning, to plan a funeral that is laced with doctrine and Gospel principles.

7. In planning a funeral, care should be taken to select people who understand what discipleship is all about so that they can honor the deceased with those things that are most important in life and death.

Chapter Seventeen
Summary

So when this corruptible shall have put on incorruption, and this mortal shall have put on immortality, then shall be brought to pass the saying that is written, Death is swallowed up in victory.

O death, where is thy sting? O grave, where is thy victory?

The sting of death is sin; and the strength of sin is the law.

But thanks be to God, which giveth us the victory through our Lord Jesus Christ.

Therefore, my beloved brethren, be ye stedfast, unmoveable, always abounding in the work of the Lord, forasmuch as ye know that your labour is not in vain in the Lord

1 Corinthians 15:54-58

The writing of this book has been an informative and testimony building journey. I have learned a great deal in researching and discovering the bedrock doctrines pertaining to life and death as taught by apostles and prophets. I have seen an increase in my own personal testimony as I have contemplated the truths which I have learned while writing this book. One of the most important of these truths which has come to me over and over again has to do with Heavenly Father's love for us as manifested clearly in His great Plan of Salvation and Happiness. The fact that He has condescended to allow us to progress and grow and eventually live with Him brings inexpressible joy. What little inconvenience death involves pales when we contemplate the great happiness we may be privileged to enjoy as a result of His love!

In this last chapter, I would like to summarize some of the most important teachings which I have discovered as I have worked my way through the various chapters. The most important discovery not that this is new to me or you, is that doctrine (the firm foundation of the teachings of Jesus Christ) is where we find most comfort when we must face the challenges of life which come to us frequently and sometimes harshly. Doctrine is the greatest source of comfort when death takes a loved one. So often we are prone to focus attention on our behavior and not link that behavior to doctrine. When this happens, we are forever searching for comfort but unable to find it. I say again as I have repeatedly said in the pages of this book, the best source of comfort as we work our way through mortality is found in the doctrines of the Kingdom of God as explained by our prophet leaders.

All through mortality, we must face adversity—suffering, trials and tribulation. Without question, the most painful adversity we face is the death of a loved one. President Harold B. Lee believed that the death of a loved one is life's most "severe test," indeed the most difficult experience of all mortal experiences. President Lee had to face this and it is likely all of us will at some point in time. I add confidently that when we are armed with true doctrine as found in the Church of Jesus Christ of Latter-day Saints, we will find the courage, the determination, and the strength to pass life's most severe test. We all know that there is no escaping what some people frighteningly call death or the "angel of death" or the "grim reaper."[103] There is no way also that we can escape the severe test that is associated with death.

I started this book by reminding us all that mortality is but a fleeting moment in the vast expanse of eternity; it is a nanosecond when we contemplate how short our time is in this mortal sphere compared with the never-ending vastness of eternity. In this brief moment in the eternal scheme of things, we live our lives, work our way through mortality and come to know that at some point in time we are going to die. Indeed, we surely were born and death is not far behind. We are

---

103   The "grim reaper" is sometimes referred to in Biblical context as the "angel of death" as, for example, when death came upon Egypt's first born sons.

all born to die; we cannot escape mortality without going through the process of death.

But just as all of us are born to die, so too, all of us are destined to live again through the blessing of the infinite Atonement of our Savior Jesus Christ. The Atonement, as we know, provides two incomprehensible blessings. The first is universal resurrection, meaning that everyone who has come to mortal existence will enjoy immortality. All who have walked the paths of mortality will become immortal when the spirit and the body are eventually reunited. The second incomprehensible blessing, for those who have desired to keep the commandments of our Father and His Son and honor sacred covenants which they have entered into, is to grow and develop and eventually enjoy eternal life and increase in His presence. All of this is brought about by the Atonement of our Savior.

A friend, Sherry Barrus[104], recently impressed me deeply with a talk on the Atonement. Her thoughtful talk summed up the far reaching power of the Atonement. She said, among many other important things:

> If there had been no Atonement of Christ (there having been a fall of Adam), then the whole plan and purpose connected with the creation of man would have come to naught. If there had been no Atonement, temporal death would have remained forever and there never would have been a resurrection. The body would have remained forever in the grave and the spirit would have stayed in a spirit prison for all eternity. If there had been no Atonement, there never would have been spiritual or eternal life for any persons. Neither mortals nor spirits could have been cleansed from sin, and all the spirit hosts of heaven would have wound up as devils, angels to a devil, that is as sons of perdition (2 Nephi 9:6-9; D&C 29:39-41).

With these great promised blessings which we derive from the Atonement, why would we "stand in awe of death," or shrink from the test which death of a loved one brings? Why would we not rejoice

---

104   Sister Barrus impressed me deeply with her insights pertaining to the Atonement. I express appreciation here for her thoughtful presentation which is available upon request.

at such elevating eventualities? What the severe test brings to faithful people is an understanding and faith in the atoning sacrifice of our Savior and because of it we don't need to stand in awe of death. And when we don't, we are well on our way to passing life's most severe test.

From the Prophet Joseph Smith we learn most of the doctrines pertaining to life and death (please see Chapter Five). I mention only two here to not only refresh our memories of what the Prophet said about them, but also to be comforted by them. It should come as no surprise to us that our great advantage in this mortal world is that we derive our faith and knowledge from true doctrine taught by prophets and apostles.

In the King Follett funeral sermon (April 7, 1844), the Prophet taught that:

> God Himself was once as we are now and is an exalted man—He has form like a man.

> Think about that! We can become like our Father in Heaven—our future progress is virtually unlimited. What a future is before us!

The Prophet also taught:

> We must learn to become gods ourselves—learning, progressing eventually to sit on thrones in everlasting power.[105]

What comfort prophetic doctrine is as the faithful Saints continue their march through mortality.

In life and in death, we must face many adversities (including death) which we are called upon to endure. But, we have learned in the pages of this book that in reality, "adversity is a treasure and scarce any man hath enough of it."[106] Adversity can teach us so much of life's important lessons which, I'm sorry to say, we can learn in no other way. In a sense, every experience we have in life is a learning experience and, in most cases, we know that experience can be a great teacher.

---

105   See the King Follett Sermon in Chapter Five.
106   At the beginning of Chapter Eight, please see the poem by John Donne from whence these lines were taken.